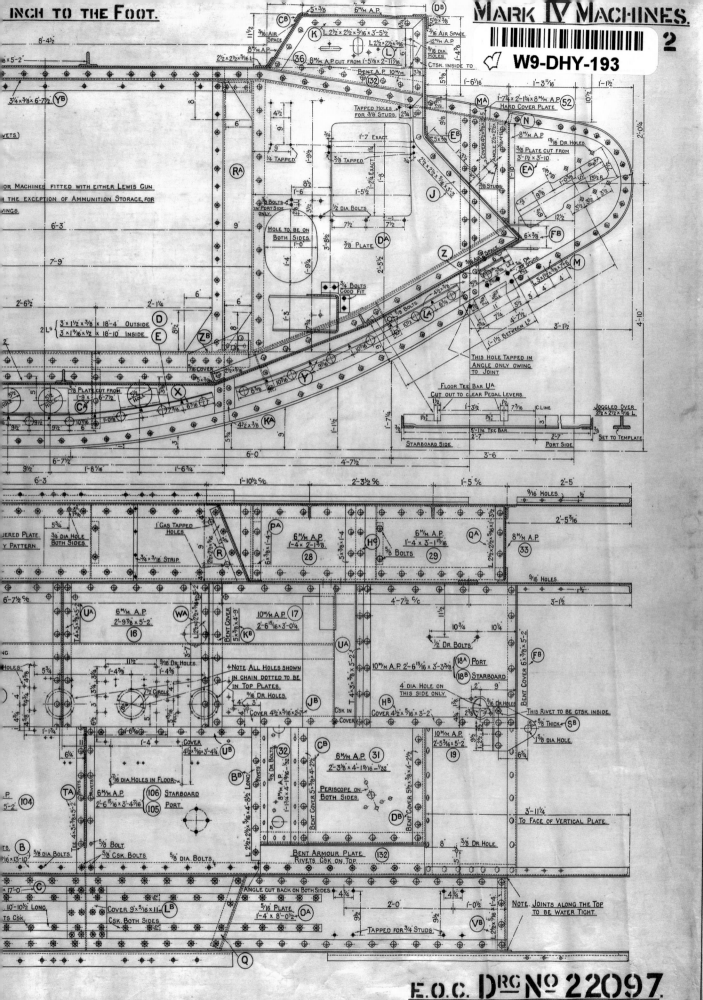

INCH TO THE FOOT.

E.O.C. DRG No. 22097.

GREAT WAR TANK

COVER CUTAWAY: **Mark IV Tank.** *(Ian Moores)*

ENDPAPERS: **The plans for the Mark IV from the archives of the Tank Museum.**

NOTE: **All of the archive photographs and illustrations that appear in this book are from the Tank Museum collection. Modern colour photography is by Matt Sampson.**

First published in 2013

A catalogue record for this book is available from the British Library

ISBN 978 085733 242 4

Library of Congress control no. 2012948590

Published by Haynes Publishing,
Sparkford, Yeovil,
Somerset BA22 7JJ, UK.
Tel: 01963 442030 Fax: 01963 440001
Int. tel: +44 1963 442030 Int. fax: +44 1963 440001
E-mail: sales@haynes.co.uk
Website: www.haynes.co.uk

Haynes North America Inc.,
861 Lawrence Drive, Newbury Park,
California 91320, USA.

Printed in the USA by Odcombe Press LP,
1299 Bridgestone Parkway, La Vergne, TN 37086.

GREAT WAR TANK

Mark IV

Haynes

THE **TANK** MUSEUM

Owners' Workshop Manual

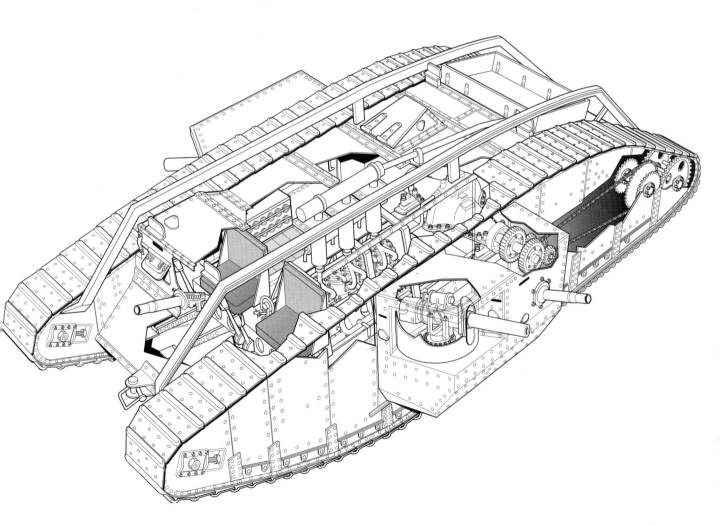

An insight into the history, development, production and role of the main British Army tank of the First World War

David Fletcher

Additional material by David Willey with photography by Matt Sampson

Contents

OPPOSITE The Mark IV replica at the Tank Museum. The fear induced by the approach of such a machine in battle can be well imagined.

Prologue

To a modern soldier, used to the technical complexity of a 21st-century main battle tank like Challenger 2, the Mark IV looks and feels positively prehistoric. Eight men inside a riveted, armoured box, clustered around a hot and noisy engine in a fume-laden atmosphere is like an image from hell. When they learn that the machine has no sprung suspension at all, a top speed of just over 3mph, and a gunsight on a male tank that is little more than a graduated telescope, these modern soldiers simply cannot grasp how anyone could survive, let alone fight and overcome, in such dreadful conditions.

What they fail to understand, of course, is that in 1917 the Mark IV tank was the latest thing, the cutting edge of modern technology, and the men who formed its crew were hailed as warriors of a new, technological age. Not only that, it demanded skills that the average soldier could only achieve under good and thorough instruction. Indeed, by 1917 it would be fair to say that a well-trained tank soldier knew more about the mechanism of his tank and how to fix it in an emergency, than his modern counterpart could ever hope to do. But in those early days it was a matter of life or death; if their tank broke down it was up to the crew to put it right – they had no means of calling for assistance.

In the end, though, it all comes down to training, and it is likely that the soldier of today and his counterpart from the First World War could swap places easily because, fundamentally, their dedication to the job is identical. Given that people don't actually change that much it seems to be a reasonable supposition. In these pages you will meet such people, the kind who, when their own tank breaks down, simply walk across to another abandoned tank nearby, remove the parts that have broken on their own tank, and then drive it home. Indeed, some of the surviving accounts are positively breathtaking. Take, for example, the crew of F24, *Frisky II*, at Cambrai in November 1917:

'Proceeded under heavy machine-gun fire towards Flot Farm. Finding the infantry were unable to follow, the Tank returned, and was directed by the infantry to attack certain strong points. After firing at these and not silencing them, Tank returned to the infantry and took on board an officer and six other ranks to bomb the strong points, whilst the tank stood by. One was visited and no enemy reported. On account of lack of petrol Tank had to return, and was hand-fed through the carburettor from three spare tins of petrol carried inside the Tank, as it was impossible to obtain access to the petrol tank. Later the Tank was refilled and returned to the rallying point.' *(The History of the Sixth Tank Battalion, 1919).*

Just imagine hand feeding the carburettor from petrol cans carried *inside* the tank, under fire, because it was too dangerous to get out and refill the main petrol tank at the back. The whole thing could have gone up in flames at any moment. And that is the story of just one tank among hundreds.

Of course, there is another side to this. Today's young officers, shown the Cambrai battlefield, often remark that an area of ground which in 1917 would be filled with tanks from an entire battalion – that is to say nearly 50 machines – could now easily be dominated by a pair of modern main battle tanks such as

BELOW Captain Reggie Lyles, MC, and his crew from A Battalion with their female tank at the Rollencourt Tankodrome in 1917.

Challenger 2s on account of their speed, plus the range and accuracy of their guns. Which means that in effect one regiment of Challenger 2 tanks could probably achieve more, over that same battlefield, as nine battalions of Mark IVs could have done in 1917, so there has been considerable progress since.

The Battle of Cambrai features largely in the *Great War Tank Manual*, as indeed it should; it was a significant event in the First World War that heavily involved the Mark IV tank and saw the operational use of many unusual modifications that have been included in these pages. However, it would be wrong to ignore the impact of the tank on the earlier Third Battle of Ypres. Dismissed by most contemporaries as a misuse of tanks – and described by J.F.C. Fuller as 'a complete study of how to move thirty tons of metal through a morass of mud and water' and characterised by Captain Basil Liddell Hart as 'Maltreatment' – the official opinion, summed up in the British Official History, was that 'Although many tanks were ditched or slithered into deep shell-craters as they rumbled to the battlefield, nineteen of this echelon overtook the infantry and gave valuable assistance in gaining the second objective.'

In fact, the number of tanks deployed at Third Ypres was not that inferior to those fielded at Cambrai and, as the section on Operation Hush shows, it was not without innovation. It also included certain striking highlights such as the relatively minor but eminently successful tank operation against the German strongpoints around St Julien in August 1917, described in

detail by Douglas Browne in *The Tank in Action* (William Blackwood, 1920). Appalling as they were, the conditions around Ypres proved to be a severe test of men and machines so far as the Tank Corps was concerned, and the fact that they came through it in good condition and in time to put up a supreme performance at Cambrai suggests that in many respects Third Ypres was the trial the Tank Corps had to pass through to make it fit for the future. As such it should not be dismissed out of hand nor its achievements ignored.

However, there is a case for enquiring into the logic behind the adoption of the Mark IV tank in the first place. An improved type, at least in terms of transmission, had already been trialled and accepted before the first Mark IV entered service, giving rise to the claim from many quarters that Albert Stern had cluttered the production facilities and the Army up with large numbers of cumbersome and out of date tanks just when better ones were urgently needed. There is some truth in this, although it ignores the relatively low status of the tank in the production hierarchy, the inherent limitations in the production cycle, along with such factors as politics and personalities.

Whether such matters have any place in a book such as this is debatable since this is primarily a technical treatise, and with restricted space these issues have not been pursued here. Anyone wishing to do so will find an enlightening if somewhat biased account in *TANKS 1914–1918, The Log-Book of a Pioneer* by Sir Albert Stern (Hodder & Stoughton, London, 1919).

ABOVE Challenger 2. This tank is used by the Armoured Trials and Development Unit based at Bovington to test new upgrades and improvements. Bovington was selected as the location to train British tank crews in the First World War and remains the home of British tank training today.

Introduction

The city of Lincoln is the birthplace of the tank, but present-day visitors would be hard pressed to find very much evidence of this. True one can still see the engraved brass plate on the door of the Yarborough Room at the White Hart Hotel, recording the fact that here, William Tritton and Walter Wilson did much of the design work on the very first tank, known as *Mother*. And in the Museum of Lincolnshire Life one can see a Mark IV female tank, a typical example of the most significant type of British tank from the First World War, although it was not in fact built in Lincoln.

Digging deeper the results are disappointing. Visiting the New Boultham district of Lincoln will reveal a Tritton Road, if one knows who Tritton was, and some locals can show a length of wall, which is all that seems to remain of the Wellington Foundry, the home of William Foster & Co. Ltd, where some of the tanks were built – but that is just about all.

William Foster began his business career in Lincoln as a miller but he had a strong bent towards engineering and in due course the firm began to manufacture agricultural and milling equipment. When Foster died in 1876, fortunately there was a strongly motivated board in place and in 1900 they built a new factory on Firth Road, New Boultham, to which they transferred the title Wellington Foundry. In 1905 they appointed a new and dynamic general manager.

William Ashbee Tritton was born in 1875. He had an impressive background in engineering, but by accepting this post at Foster's, at a relatively early age he was also accepting a massive challenge. Foster's was never going to be an industrial giant but Tritton established the company's name abroad, particularly in South America, and he also gradually modernised the firm, reducing its reliance on steam in favour of a range of internal combustion tractors. It was this expertise that brought Foster's to the attention of the Admiralty and subsequently the War Office.

On 29 July 1915 William Tritton, who was in London, accepted a contract to build a prototype 'Landship' and telegraphed Foster's;

RIGHT **William Ashbee Tritton, managing director of Foster's, who was credited with the invention of the track.**

FAR RIGHT **Walter Gordon Wilson, in the uniform of a major in the Tank Corps. Wilson came up with the concept of the rhomboid shape of the tank. Both he and Tritton were rewarded for inventing the tank by the Royal Commission on Awards to Inventors in 1919.**

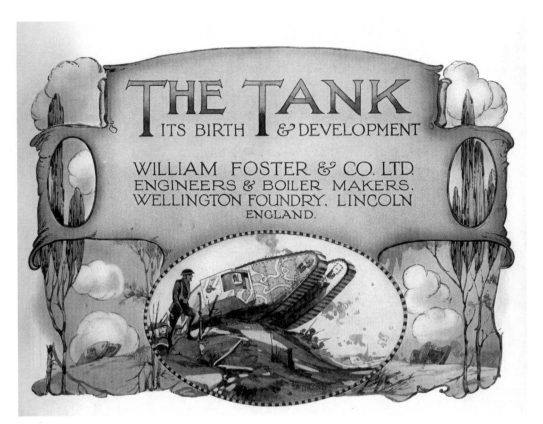

part of his message read: 'Whole Landship job handed to us with Wilson as Overseer. He and Legros coming to Lincoln. Ask Starkey to start more draughtsmen if possible. Will wire after further interview with D'Eyncourt this afternoon.'

Wilson was Lieutenant Walter Gordon Wilson, RNAS, a testy man but something of an inventive genius, although his duties at this time involved acting as Admiralty supervisor at Lincoln. Lucien Legros was an old friend of Colonel R.E.B. Crompton who, for the previous five months as technical adviser to the Admiralty Landships Committee, had developed a range of prototypes on his drawing board. The most recent of which was about to be constructed, although a number of firms that had originally agreed to build it had run into difficulties and excused themselves from the task. Foster's had agreed to take it on, but since Crompton was being relieved of his duties his design would never see the light of day, and it is not entirely clear what part Legros was likely to play in future developments – in the event, probably none. James Starkey, who was then Foster's chief draughtsman, would become the company's technical director in 1917, his earlier position passing to William Rigby

who, in effect, was already deeply involved in the Landships project, having been loaned to Crompton in an effort to speed things up. Eustace Tennyson D'Eyncourt was the Admiralty's Director of Naval Construction who, somewhat against his better judgement, had

been coerced by Winston Churchill to supervise the entire project as chairman of the Admiralty Landships Committee.

Once the contract with Foster's was drawn up, Tritton again cabled the firm from London in order to get them started, in part reading 'take a Daimler set and build it into a box such as Rigby drew'. The Daimler set, of course, was the 105hp Daimler–Knight six-cylinder engine, clutch, gearbox and differential that was then being installed in the Foster–Daimler tractor, but the 'box such as Rigby drew' – what was that? The conclusion is that it must be something to do with the time Rigby spent with Crompton in London, in which case one might say that Crompton had, at least vicariously, some input into the first design to come from Foster's.

History is always easier to absorb when it follows a nice, steady progression, but experience teaches us that this is rarely the case in reality. Thus it is well to keep in mind that while Tritton, Wilson and the staff at Foster's were creating their prototype machine, usually referred to as the Number One Lincoln Machine, experiments were still being pursued at Burton upon Trent with alternative designs such as the articulated Bullock tractors, which represented the end of the Landship project under Colonel Crompton.

Colonel Rookes Evelyn Bell Crompton, one of the most venerable engineers of his day, whose military background entitled him to wear medals acquired during the Crimean and Boer Wars, had been seconded to Churchill's Admiralty Landships Committee early in 1915. He became a convinced supporter of the articulated Landship concept and had gone along with the fundamental change in emphasis from a troop carrier, as envisaged by the Admiralty pioneers, to a turreted fighting vehicle, as subsequently required by the War Office. Even so this was all somewhat insubstantial since Crompton seemed unable to deliver the precise drawings that engineering companies required, so up to the summer of 1915 nothing had actually been built except for a wooden mock-up.

Meanwhile, a selection of items was being delivered from subcontractors and, as the complexities of the design were being appreciated, the primary contractor was getting cold feet. The Patent Shaft and Axletree Co. Ltd of Wednesbury, part of the Metropolitan Carriage, Wagon & Finance Company, had been appointed main contractor in the middle of April when Fodens of Sandbach in Cheshire, Crompton's first choice, had been forced to relinquish it due to industrial trouble. Patent Shaft soon became disillusioned with the project but agreed to continue for a while until in July 1915 Eustace Tennyson D'Eyncourt decided to transfer the contract to William Foster & Co.

At which point things get a mite complicated. Crompton soon learned that Foster's had been requested to begin by constructing a half-Landship, only going on to build the full articulated type later. Crompton was understandably upset and wrote a letter casting aspersions on Tritton's abilities as an engineer, but when he realised that Tritton and Wilson between them were working on a different design, based around a single Daimler engine, he was mortified. It implied a rough-and-ready approach rather than his engineering refinement.

The chances are that Foster's would never have built a Crompton Landship, either an articulated one or a half unit, because Crompton was still unable to produce adequate drawings, but in any case it seems clear that Stern was relying on Tritton and Wilson quickly to come up with a workable design, having run out of patience with the cautious, pedantic Crompton and his Victorian ways. Yet unbiased observers might concede that there is a distinct similarity between Crompton's later design and the machine that ultimately became *Little Willie* – at least in outward appearance.

Work on the Tritton–Wilson design began at the Wellington Foundry on 11 August and it was completed, up to a point, by 8 September. However, both Tritton and Wilson knew that as it stood, with an unmodified length of Bullock track flat to the ground, it was never going to work.

Even so, an attempt was made to drive it out into Foster's yard the next day but it was clearly quite hopeless. As Tritton and Wilson recognised, a length of unsprung track should ideally present a curved surface to the ground or it would be impossible to steer. Tritton put the necessary modifications in hand so that the vehicle was ready to roll ten days later, on 19 September 1915.

The location chosen for the new demonstration was an area of land adjacent to Cross O' Cliff Hill about two kilometres away; among those who witnessed this trial was George Field, who had been Crompton's emissary in the United States, and Ernest Swinton, a British Army officer and an avid supporter of the Landship idea who, in ignorance of the Admiralty's project, had been ploughing his own furrow in the same direction.

In fact, despite Tritton's modifications the vehicle still did not perform very well, shedding its tracks every time it tackled an obstacle and finishing up disabled to the point where it took two days to repair it and drive it back to the factory. George Field inspected the machine and soon understood what was wrong. The people at Foster's had failed to use some of the material sent over from Chicago, despite detailed instructions for its use, so in his view failure was inevitable. And it was probably true; neither Tritton nor Wilson had any faith in the American tracks and in any case they were in a hurry. Both men realised that only a different style of track would be fit for purpose and Wilson had already come up with the idea of an all-round track design for which a new type of track would be required anyway. Perhaps they had even planned it this way. Field also claimed that the new machine was too slow and blamed this on the fact that Tritton and Wilson installed the Daimler engine and gearbox back to front, with the result that the machine had just one forward gear and two reverse. It would have been perfectly simple to correct this but it is unclear whether or not it was done. It may have served as yet another stick with which Field could beat Tritton and Wilson.

BELOW William Tritton was knighted on 13 February 1917 and is seen on the extreme right of this picture, taken on 2 March 1918. The occasion was the visit of General Sir William Robertson to Foster's. The two figures at the other end of the line are J. Starkey and C.W. Pennel.

Chapter One

The tank story

The invention of the tank was one of the great dramas of the First World War. It was an entirely new invention created from virtually nothing, yet it went almost straight into production and active service. Obviously they were not all perfect, and improvements were continually being investigated.

OPPOSITE A view inside the erecting shop at Foster's Wellington Foundry at Lincoln with Mark IV tanks under construction. Both tanks in the foreground show the original envelope radiator. The photograph contains a lot of interesting detail.

Design and Building of the Mark IV

Origins

If one regards the Mark IV tank as the first production type, and its predecessors Marks I, II and III as prototypes, that is not far from the truth. The idea of a Landship capable of overcoming the prevailing conditions on the Western Front is attributed to Winston Churchill, the First Lord of the Admiralty. Experimentation was carried out by Royal Naval personnel and the cost borne entirely by the Admiralty budget. Unfortunately they were following the wrong line of approach, devising a Landship to carry a party of infantry over the fire-swept

ABOVE *Little Willie* seen towards the end of the war in the mud at Dollis Hill. By this time it had been relegated to the category of relic, albeit a venerated one.

BELOW *Little Willie* survives as an exhibit in the Tank Museum at Bovington. Notice how the bottom run of track describes a gentle curve when it stands on hard ground.

LITTLE WILLIE
~1915~

zone of no-man's-land, over the barbed wire to the enemy trenches, where they would then dismount and go into action in the traditional way; what would be described today as an armoured personnel carrier.

When the War Office took over in the early summer of 1915 they had different ideas. They wanted a fighting vehicle capable of crushing the wire and crossing trenches, but also equipped with weapons that could be discharged on the move to provide infantry with immediate fire support right up to its final objective, and with some degree of protection against a counter-attack thereafter.

The Admiralty had invested a lot of faith in their resident expert, Colonel Rookes Evelyn Bell Crompton, who had been a staunch advocate of an articulated vehicle and who, in an effort to accommodate the War Office, had adapted his designs to carry a turret while still retaining the concept of the articulated type, which by this time was becoming increasingly complicated.

The story of how Crompton's design was adapted by two more realistic and commercially astute engineers is too convoluted to relate here, but the immediate result was a crude vehicle nicknamed *Little Willie*, which was fitted with a new design of track devised by one member of the team, William Ashbee Tritton, managing director of William Foster & Co. of Lincoln, agricultural engineers. His partner,

Walter Gordon Wilson, then saw the potential of this track and used it to create an altogether new design, roughly rhomboidal in shape, with the tracks running clear around the outside, which at one stroke solved the problems of trench crossing and driving over uneven and shelled ground. Wilson's design, known as *Big Willie* or *Mother* was built at Foster's using Tritton's track, where it first saw the light of day on 6 January 1916.

Trials in Burton Park, Lincoln, and Hatfield Park, Hertfordshire, served to convince the great and the good that here was a device worth trying and before long a requirement for 150 was established, the first of which were transported to France and ready for action by the middle of September 1916; going from untried prototype to battle-worthy weapon in just over nine months.

Even so, there was no use pretending that this first design was perfect. The Mark I tank, as it later became known, was effectively obsolete by the following summer. It required numerous improvements, from the thickness of the armour to the configuration of sponsons and weapons and the fuel supply, most of which were integrated gradually into the blueprint of its successors Marks II and III and ultimately incorporated with others into the more successful Mark IV that is described here. Design work on the Mark IV is said to

have begun in October 1916 and the plans attributed to W.A. Tritton and W.G. Wilson, as is logical. The order that established production of the Mark IV in substantial numbers was not without its complications, due in part to the personalities and prejudices of those involved – notably Albert Stern of the Tank Supply Department, supported by the Commander-in-Chief in France, Sir Douglas Haig, and David Lloyd George, Minister of Munitions – and opposed by reactionary elements at the War Office who appeared to resent Stern's methods and the entire concept of a new weapon designed by civilians for which they could see no requirement. When finally established the order amounted to 1,220 Mark IVs of all types. The lion's share by the Metropolitan Carriage,

ABOVE *Mother* **tackling a succession of obstacles in Burton Park, Lincoln, in January 1916. Tritton, far right in the bowler, and Wilson, on the edge of the picture, observe proceedings.**

BELOW A Mark I male tank, with its sponsons removed, climbs aboard a railway wagon at Foster's yard in Lincoln.

24 April 1918 and Mark IVs that were selected to participate in the first amphibious operation involving tanks landing from the sea. And it was the Mark IVs – 476 of them in fighting and ancillary roles – which swept across the rolling downland west of Cambrai on 20 November 1917, and delivered momentarily the vision of ultimate success and victory. Other tanks designed using knowledged gained from the Mark IV appeared later, and were faster, easier to drive and more reliable, but none went through the experiences that the Mark IV and its crews did.

Mark IV tank production

The manufacturers that built Mark IV tanks in the First World War can be divided into three categories. First come the major contractors who assembled complete tanks. Foremost of these was the Metropolitan Carriage, Wagon & Finance Company, which ultimately constructed 640 male and female fighting tanks plus 180 tenders, or supply tanks; the assembly lines for these were set up at one of their constituent companies, the Oldbury Railway Carriage & Wagon Co. Ltd. The other major contractor was William Foster & Co. Ltd, who was responsible for assembling 100 Mark IV male tanks. Rather than building from the beginning with raw materials, they took delivery of a kit of components and from it fabricated complete tanks. These kits included armour plate cut to size, drilled for riveting and heat treated to become bullet proof, engine and gearbox assemblies from Daimler of Coventry and in the case of male tanks, six-pounder guns from Armstrong, Whitworth on Tyneside.

The next category comprises firms who put together tanks that had already been part assembled by someone else, such as Sir W.G. Armstrong, Whitworth Ltd, who undertook to deliver 100 male tanks, and three companies in Scotland, specifically in Glasgow, these being the Coventry Ordnance Works (100 female), Mirrlees, Watson & Co. (50 female) and William Beardmore & Co. Ltd (25 female and 25 tenders). However, these firms invariably took delivery of assembled hulls and completed them at their own plants. Among those who simply riveted up hulls were the North British Locomotive Company and the rolling stock

Wagon & Finance Company through their Oldbury subsidiary but others, to the tune of 50 or 100 by William Foster & Co. of Lincoln, Sir W.G. Armstrong, Whitworth & Co. Ltd in Gateshead, Mirrlees Watson Co. Ltd, the Coventry Ordnance Works Ltd and William Beardmore & Co. Ltd, all of Glasgow. However, it is fair to point out that the advent of the tank imposed tremendous demands on the supply of materials, manufacturing capacity and the demand for skilled labour at a time when its potential was an unknown quantity. Not that this was the end of the story, as better and more sophisticated designs were already in service by the time the war ended, but the Mark IV was there too, having carried the war to the enemy through the crucial year of 1917 and in diminishing numbers thereafter. It was a Mark IV tank that took part on the British side in the very first tank versus tank action near Cachy on

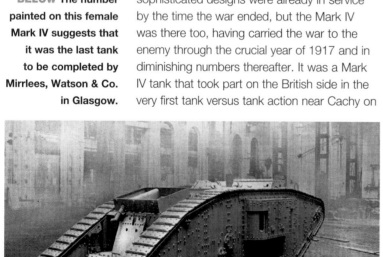

ABOVE LEFT A poor print showing tanks in various stages of construction in the William Beardmore factory at Dalmuir, west of Glasgow.

ABOVE A closer look at a Beardmore's tank under construction; notice the shafts extending from the idler and sprocket openings at each end, used to align the hull plates.

LEFT A new Mark IV female from Beardmore's on its first outing. There is evidence of new building all around.

BELOW LEFT It is interesting to see that new tanks being built at Beardmore's do not appear to have been given numbers; at least none are visible.

BELOW Glasgow rolling-stock manufacturers Hurst Nelson assembled hulls of Mark IV tanks, although how they were delivered is not explained.

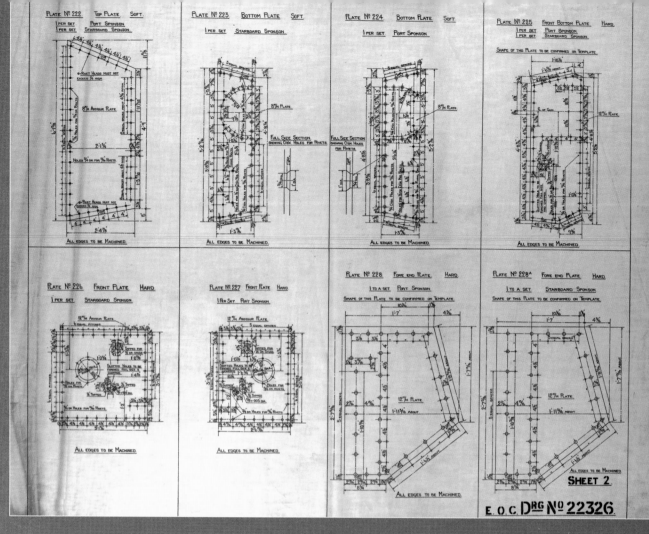

E.O.C. D^{RG} N^O 22326.

ARMOUR PLATE

ABOVE Plans for the armour plate.

BELOW A diagram showing the arrangement of hull plates on a Mark IV male tank.

According to a letter from the English Steel Corporation to the Tank Museum Curator in 1967 the plate was a nickel chrome composition roughly equivalent to the IT.70 standard of the Second World War, described as Homogeneous Hard Armour. The armouring process involved first cutting and drilling the plate in its soft state and then subjecting it to a heating process before finally being quenched in a press between two cold-water-filled containers. This created plates of different thickness of 6mm, 8mm and 12mm, which were distributed on a typical tank as follows. Maximum thickness (12mm plate) was primarily located to protect the crew and 8mm plate was considered sufficient to safeguard the engine and mechanical parts while 6mm was provided for the pressed-steel track plates. The armour plate was regarded as proof against rifle and machine guns firing conventional bullets, from shrapnel and grenade fragments.

Recent examination of a badly corroded piece of 6mm plate from a First World War tank by the Centre for Materials Science and Engineering at Cranfield University revealed a low steel alloy of chrome, nickel and molybdenum, which required heat treating at 850 degrees centigrade for 30 minutes and then quench-hardened to produce a face-hardened surface.

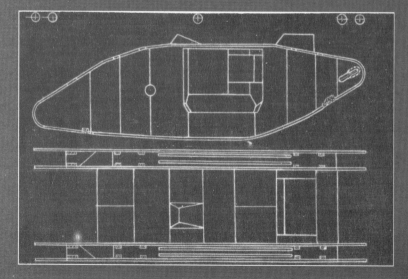

manufacturer Hurst, Nelson & Company. Whether there were others and how the hulls were moved from one site to another has yet to be discovered. The exception may be Beardmore's, who claim to have built tanks from scratch at their Dalmuir facility on the Clyde.

The third category consists of those firms that manufactured tank components such as the Daimler Company Ltd of Coventry who supplied the 105hp engine, flywheel, clutch, gearbox and differential all mounted on its own rigid girder chassis for immediate installation into the hull of the tank; Sir W.G. Armstrong, Whitworth Ltd of Newcastle who made and supplied the 57mm six-pounder guns for male tanks; and the steelmakers, William Beardmore Ltd, at their Parkhead works in Glasgow, and two Sheffield-based firms, Vickers Ltd and Cammell Laird. Of these, Beardmore's were in the most unusual position; in the first place they had been involved, as early as 1914, with the development of thin armour plate for the Royal Naval Air Service for their armoured cars. Also, as already noted, the firm had been contracted to build 50 tanks. Beardmore's also produced six-pounder tank guns in their Ordnance Department at Parkhead and proof-tested them on their Proof Range at Inchterff, some ten miles from Glasgow. However, since Beardmore's themselves only ever built female and supply tanks these guns must have been delivered to other firms. Beardmore's also list track links and ball mountings for tank machine guns among their products.

Although Foster's of Lincoln also produced track links, other engineering firms were involved, for example Clayton & Shuttleworth, another Lincoln firm that also made track links, while in their wartime souvenir publication Ruston & Hornsby Ltd – then still trading in Lincoln as Ruston, Proctor & Co. Ltd during the war – indicate that they produced male sponsons for Mark IV tanks and mountings for the six-pounder gun, although whether for use in tanks is not entirely clear.

Two problems arose that affected tank production. The first was a shortage in the supply of track links. As demand for tanks and spare parts increased it was realised that the original design, which used cast-steel links, could not keep pace so a new version, made

by the drop-forge process, was introduced. This, however, brought troubles of its own since the drop-forge technique was not properly understood by some contractors or their employees. The other difficulty concerned the supply of weapons. Originally the contractors had just about kept up with demand by producing six-pounder guns at the rate of 360 per month, but a new programme to build two-pounder guns ate into this so that six-pounder production dropped to only 200 per month. It is probably safe to say that this did not affect Mark IV construction as such but it would certainly have been felt later on.

Tank manufacture proceeded along the usual production-line arrangements of the time with the tanks placed in rows along the factory floor. The first stage involved riveting the inner and outer frames to the floor plates and including front panels, while the roof, which was attached by bolts rather than rivets, and a rear panel which was riveted, were not fitted until the engine and transmission had been installed. Long shafts were temporarily inserted through some of the main bearing holes to ensure alignment of the frames until the hull structure was finished.

The automotive components consisting of the engine, flywheel, clutch, primary gearbox and differential were supplied complete on a subframe, which was also extended forwards to include a cross-member for the driver's seat and driving controls, and rearwards to support the radiator and cooling fan assembly. This was then lowered by overhead crane through the

BELOW An illustration from the company souvenir book showing male sponsons assembled by Ruston, Proctor & Co. of Lincoln. These would have been heavy and awkward things to handle.

open roof of the tank, bolted into place and connected up; that done the hull was entire.

Production of Mark IV tanks was not finally completed until October 1918 by which time the type was considered to be out of date; this meant that many of those built towards the end would never have been issued and were probably scrapped in 'as-new' condition.

Variants

Mark IVA

There is no doubt that the transmission of the Mark IV, evolved directly from the Mark I, was crude, labour intensive and slow. The tank had to halt in order to change gear or make a significant turn and was in any case painfully slow, limited by the power output of the Daimler engine and the low gear ratios. Indeed, Douglas Browne of G Battalion, quoting unnamed pessimists in his book *The Tank in Action*, reckoned that the transmission absorbed 75% of the available horsepower, although this is probably an exaggeration and in any case what matters most when it comes to power is the torque delivered by the engine rather than the horsepower.

Many already recognised these problems and Albert Stern initiated a programme of alternative drive systems, culminating in a competitive trial of many of the contenders at the Oldbury testing ground in March 1917. Since this was before the first Mark IV had been delivered, the competing tanks were mostly adapted Mark II machines taken straight off the production line and suitably modified. The majority of designs on offer were either too complicated or too unwieldy to work in the confined space of a tank's hull, but the system devised by W.G. Wilson appears to have been entirely suitable: drive passed from the engine, through a primary gearbox to simple epicyclic gears in the track frames resulting in what was, in effect, a workable clutch and brake steering system that could be operated by one man, the driver.

As for power, and overlooking the 125hp version of the Daimler engine for the moment, Albert Stern, having failed to persuade the Daimler Company to design a more powerful engine, turned to the gifted designer Harry Ricardo who, despite a small catalogue of limitations and conditions, succeeded in producing a six-cylinder engine which could develop 150hp and still fit inside a Mark IV tank in place of the Daimler unit.

There was a plan to rework Mark IV tanks to the Ricardo–Wilson configuration as the Mark IVA but, under the circumstances, it was deemed to be more trouble than it was worth and it was agreed to complete manufacture of the Mark IV in its original form and then begin production of a new model, the Mark V with the Ricardo engine, Wrigley gearbox and Wilson transmission. A few Mark IV tanks were converted to this Mark IVA specification but they would have been no more than prototypes.

It is known that Ricardo designed his engine to directly replace the Daimler unit in the Mark IV, but the experience with the 125hp Daimler suggests that the original transmission would not be able to handle it. Although there was a scheme developed at the end of the war to install the Wilson transmission into the Mark IV while retaining the Daimler engine, this project was simply overtaken by events when the war ended.

Stretched Mark IV

The German Siegfriednetwork of defences, known to the Allies as the Hindenburg Line, was constructed over the winter of 1916/17. It extended as far as possible along high ground in the rear of the existing German front line and was clearly the result of experience on the Somme. It was primarily a defensive position designed to be garrisoned by a

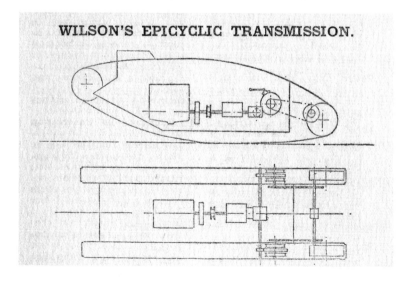

WILSON'S EPICYCLIC TRANSMISSION.

BELOW A drawing taken from the programme for the March 1917 Oldbury Trials. It shows the arrangement for a tank adapted to take a version of W.G. Wilson's epicyclic steering system but coupled to a Daimler 105hp engine. The tank, which performed, and won, at Oldbury, would have been a Mark II machine, but the composition suggested for Mark IV tanks at the end of the war would have been similar.

minimum number of troops housed in secure and relatively comfortable accommodation underground. Aware that the Allies were dedicated to evicting the invaders from France at all costs, it was intended to ensure that they would suffer the maximum number of casualties in the attempt while the defenders, remaining relatively thin on the ground, could effectively hold them at bay as the bulk of the German Army tackled the enemy in the east.

The appearance of tanks on the Western Front in September 1916 added a further dimension to this fortification. Examination of captured examples revealed that the trench-crossing potential of British tanks was limited to about 9ft, based on the original 1915 requirement, and as a result certain segments of the German defences included trenches up to 12ft wide and even more. British forces had already encountered portions of the Hindenburg Line during the attack from Arras in April 1917 and aerial reconnaissance by the Royal Flying Corps had filled in more detail subsequently. It was, by any standards, a formidable defensive position.

How to deal with this obstacle produced a number of unusual solutions. The first was the fascine (sometimes referred to as the super fascine since it was composed of 75 normal fascines), which weighed 1.75 tons. As used at Cambrai in November 1917 each tank taking part had one of these bundles of brushwood perched atop the cab and secured by chains. Each fascine was about 4ft 6in in diameter

and some 10ft in width; its purpose was to support the rear of the tank as it crossed the wider trenches to prevent it from getting stuck. However, it could only be used once: it was almost impossible to recover and in any case was something of a wreck after a succession of tanks had driven across it. In the aftermath of Cambrai, on the assumption that wider trenches were likely to become the norm, thoughts turned to means of adapting the tanks themselves, although this clearly required modifications to the existing design.

The best known of these, the Tadpole Tail, was devised at Foster's in December 1917 and offered in different lengths: 3ft, 6ft or 9ft. This last was agreed to be the most useful and sets were ordered in January 1918. As its name suggests the Tadpole Tail was a rearward extension of the track frames or horns, bringing the overall length of the tank up to 13ft 8in. The plate used to construct this part was not armoured like the rest of the vehicle but the extensions were heavily cross-braced by girders in an effort to keep them rigid. These extension pieces required 28 additional track plates on each side and 10 extra track rollers, five flanged and five unflanged, added to the frames. Since the track drive sprockets also had to be moved further back, an additional loop of Coventry chain was fitted within the Tadpole Tail frames on each side with extra intermediate sprockets, one of which was mounted on an eccentric shaft so that it could be moved to adjust the tension of the chain.

ABOVE Demonstrating the Tadpole Tail extension over a prepared trench at Foster's testing ground.

France, sometime in 1918, shows dozens of examples lying in rows on the ground but there is no evidence that they were ever used. Even though they were also adaptable to the Mark V tank, the same objections applied and the people at Central Workshops did not like them. In any event, towards the end of the war the need for longer tanks diminished as the fighting moved away from the area dominated by the Hindenburg Line and into open country where prepared trenches did not exist.

The prototype Tadpole Tail tank, based on an unnumbered Foster's-built Mark IV male was later seen at the Mechanical Warfare Department's Experimental Ground at Dollis Hill, north-west London. In some photographs it is towing a pair of sledges while in another a six-inch trench mortar can be seen, mounted between the rear horns and arranged in such a way that it could be fired over the tank.

In practice although the Tadpole Tail attachment worked, in that it enabled the tank to cross a trench up to 14ft wide without falling in the extension, it was not judged to be rigid enough, particularly when the tank was steering, so it was never adopted. A photograph taken at Central Workshops in

LEFT One experiment that took advantage of the space available at the rear of a Tadpole Tail machine is this one, which involved installing a six-inch mortar arranged to fire forwards, over the tank. It was photographed at the Dollis Hill testing ground.

BELOW Another experiment conducted at Dollis Hill involved the Tadpole Tail tank towing supply sledges. They are using the Top Towing position to keep the cables clear of the tracks. These cables run beneath the sledges, which remain in place due to friction.

LEFT This view of the Tank Corps Central Workshops at Erin, in France, shows dozens of Tadpole Tail attachments stored but never used.

Central Workshops in France clearly had their own ideas on this matter because reports survive of an experiment they conducted earlier in 1917 on instructions from Tank Corps Headquarters to create a longer tank. The task was passed to No 2 Repair Section who chopped a Mark IV tank in two, just in the rear of the sponsons, and inserted an additional 6ft of hull. Although not as long as the Tadpole Tail, it was free from the objection of flexibility since it was the body of the tank itself that was extended rather than the extremities. Where the extra plate came from is unclear but one assumes not from other wrecks at Central Workshops because such plates would not be the correct shape. No photographs have yet been found to indicate what this variant looked like but, based on similar changes to other tanks, it seems reasonable to suppose that it added at least a further four tons to the overall weight, which was bound to inhibit performance. According to Central Workshops, trench crossing was improved but steering, or 'swinging', was not due to the low horsepower of the Daimler engine. Certainly there is no evidence that the concept was proceeded with at the time. Ultimately a stretched version of the Mark V was produced, identified as the Mark V* (Mark V star), along the same lines, so in that sense the stretched Mark IV could be seen as a prototype.

Supply tanks

Supply tanks first appeared at the Battle of Messines, launched on 28 May 1917, which was the first action that saw the debut of the Mark IV tank on the battlefield. The role of each supply tank was to carry forward those consumables that five combat tanks required, such as fuel, grease and ammunition, the idea being that it saved the fighting tanks from having to drive back to their starting point to refill, which would otherwise use up precious track mileage and fuel.

At this time the supply tanks were created

BELOW A carrying party on the Ypres battlefield. Labour intensive and very tiring. A Mark IV tank lies disabled to the right.

from redundant Mark I and Mark II tanks fitted with male sponsons with the weapons removed and the apertures plated over to create room for carrying stores. The success of their service led to the creation of dedicated supply tanks and, ultimately, the creation of special supply companies.

Walter Owen Bentley, later to become famous as the designer of some impressive sports cars, was a lieutenant in the Royal Naval Air Service during the war, concentrating on aero-engine design in conjunction with squadron commander Wilfred Briggs, one of the armoured-car pioneers. Before the war, as a civilian engineer, Bentley specialised in the

development of aluminium pistons for internal combustion engines, and he was instrumental in the development of the Rolls-Royce Eagle from a Mercedes original.

The need to improve the performance of the 105hp Daimler engine in the first tanks was already recognised and, while Albert Stern tried vainly to persuade the Daimler Company to develop a more powerful engine, Bentley was invited to see what he could do with the existing one. By fitting new aluminium pistons, which increased the compression ratio from 4.2:1 to 4.75:1 and providing a new Zenith twin carburettor, Bentley managed to increase the power output from 105 to 125hp, but at the expense of creating a much more temperamental engine that did not take kindly to the harsh treatment meted out by tank crews under extreme pressure in combat. Another unfortunate side effect, a combination of greater engine power and the stress of battle, seems to have been a problem with the secondary gear shafts in the Mark IV, which could be twisted out of shape, bringing the tank to a halt on the battlefield. One source quotes the number of 125hp engines produced as 220.

It is not clear just how many regular fighting tanks were fitted with the more powerful engine but there must have been some otherwise the problem might not have been identified; it is understood, though, that 125 were completed as supply tanks, which appeared later in the war. Classed at the time as tenders, 100 were produced, in two groups, by the Metropolitan Carriage, Wagon & Finance Company, probably at their Oldbury Works, and a further 25 by William Beardmore and Company Ltd in Glasgow. And it should be stressed that these supply tanks were all newly built as such and not converted from existing fighting tanks.

These tanks are recognised primarily by their large, box-shaped sponsons of mild steel and a square hatch atop the front cab. The internal arrangements are not entirely known although it is said that wire mesh grills were provided inside the tank to prevent stores from falling against the engine. However, a certain amount can be deduced. In the first place the hatch in the cab suggests that the driver and commander had no other route in or out of the vehicle because their way to the sponson doors was blocked.

BELOW Since they
were known as supply
tanks most had
the word 'SUPPLY'
painted boldly on each
sponson. However, in
some cases the term
'BAGGAGE' was used
instead

There must have been enough space for the secondary gears-men to operate and to enable them to work the starting crank. In fact one assumes that there was adequate space, at least along the starboard side of the engine, to enable someone to reach the priming cups on the cylinders. Much more might be said – about internal communications, for example – but the foregoing illustrates the problems of research where so little hard information is available.

Surviving extracts from the diary of Lieutenant D.S. Hooper of 2nd Battalion Tank Corps suggests that he commanded a supply tank during the Ypres battle in the summer of 1917. But it is not clear whether these were of the Mark IV type or earlier models converted to the role. He lists the contents of each tank as 250 rounds of 6-pounder ammunition, 60,000 rounds of machine-gun ammunition, 300gal of petrol, 100gal of oil, 10 drums of grease, 126gal of water and 40 rations. He took his tank forward but was obliged to wait until the fighting tanks ahead of him got beyond the spot where he was to create his dump. In the event they never did, most being ditched, knocked out or forced to turn back so only the two supply tanks seem to have survived unscathed and still full of supplies.

On 6 November 1917 Hooper mentions taking a supply tank 'loaded with un-ditching rails' to Second Brigade Workshops, which suggests that these rails were being unbolted from wrecked tanks and fitted to new ones. By the time of the Battle of Cambrai, on 20 November 1917, he seems to have been promoted to Company Reconnaissance Officer in his battalion.

The armament of a supply tank was limited to a single machine gun in the front of the cab; this would have been the Lewis gun for supply tanks involved in the Cambrai battle but the Hotchkiss for those serving in 1918. Supply tanks used at Cambrai would appear to have been regular Mark IV tanks converted to the role or earlier types still in running order. In the main these seem to have been operated as part of a battalion, carrying forward supplies for their own tanks.

Another innovation for Cambrai was the supply sledge; 110 of these were demanded from Central Workshops shortly before

Cambrai, and Colonel Brockbank, in charge of the workshops, complained that in addition to a complex array of metal fittings they were obliged to acquire 70 tons of timber that had to be cut to shape and prepared. The design is not recorded in detail but appears to have been based upon similar devices developed for the abortive Operation Hush.

Each sledge was deemed capable of transporting ten tons of stores and a single tank managed three such sledges. The idea was that a sledge could be detached and left at an appointed place on the battlefield to be plundered by infantry or passing tanks as required. Very little information is recorded about them or their use, compared with many accounts of how tanks, by the end of the first day of Cambrai, were running desperately low on both fuel and ammunition, so that one imagines the fighting tanks had simply missed the sledges, or been too busy at the time to stop and reload from them.

Originally it was claimed that the sledges were pulled by supply tanks, which would make a lot of sense, but evidence now appears to show that modified fighting tanks with special towing arrangements had to be employed instead. These tanks were referred to as Top Towing vehicles. In an ideal world tanks should never be employed to tow anything; it is not good for them and inhibits their flexibility and fighting capabilities on the battlefield.

However, the potential power of a tank and its prodigious tractive effort is a dreadful temptation and tanks towing trailers have been seen all around the world at various times.

BELOW Supply sledges, hitched two at a time behind a tank, could be detached and left on the battlefield for tanks to replenish from if need be.

ABOVE A female Mark IV with the modified unditching beam rails that identify it as a Top Towing example. It is also fitted with a salvage jib and appears to be operating in a Tank Corps workshop environment.

distances. The reason was that if the tank steered or 'swung' dramatically while towing the cable tended to foul the track and cause damage.

As a result Central Workshops devised the Top Towing arrangement, which consisted of a hook attached to a resilient block on top of the roof of the tank between the trapezoid-shaped commander's hatch and the open tray, or spud box on the sloping rear part of the roof. Tie rods attached to both sides of the block ran forwards and were secured in the pistol ports on both sides of the cab, although this meant that the flaps, covering these ports, could never be closed properly when the rods were hooked in place. Another distinctive feature of these Top Towing tanks was the way that a special section was added to each unditching rail so that the beam could be employed should the need arise but not when the tank was towing. This arrangement appears to have been used for the same reason on those tanks allocated to wire pulling, which used a heavy-duty grapnel attached to the tank by cable.

In February 1918 dedicated Tank Supply Companies, five of them, were formed in Britain

BELOW Nearest the camera is a supply tank in the tank park at Rollencourt. The sponson is partly retracted.

The problem with British First World War tanks was largely their shape. Shackles, suitable for towing, had been fitted at the rear of each tank both inside and outside the horns but, while quite suitable for recovering another tank, or moving it a short distance, they did not really function well towing other loads over long

and they were all in France by the late spring and early summer. At first they seem to have been attached to particular Tank Brigades for specific operations and Major W.H.L. Watson, commanding No 4 Tank Supply Company complained of the problems involved when Mark IV supply tanks went into action in the wake of Mark V fighting tanks. He explained that they found it difficult to keep up and proposed a permanent relationship between fighting battalions and supply companies, although how this might have helped is not clear. One wonders whether the additional strain of trying to keep pace with the more modern tanks might not have aggravated the secondary gear problem again, but there is no record of this.

In due course the utility of the supply tanks seems to have become more widely recognised and the *Tank Corps Book of Honour* contains accounts of gallant deeds attributed to officers and men of the Tank Supply Companies carrying stores for the infantry, the signals, including line-laying, and the Royal Engineers. The following account, which also involves supply tanks behaving like fighting tanks, illustrates this:

Temporary 2nd Lieut. Crosbie, Donald Fraser. No. 2 Tank Supply Coy. Awarded MC.
For conspicuous gallantry and resource at Landrecies on November 4, 1918.

This officer was in charge of three tanks carrying bridging material to the lock at Landrecies. On arrival at the railway station Lieut. Crosbie, realising that the infantry were held up by a machine-gun nest on the bank of the Canal, went forward alone, and hastily reconnoitring the situation, decided that no good purpose could be served by leaving the tanks where they were, as one tank had already received a direct hit. He accordingly transferred the load from the derelict tank to a fit tank, and, under heavy shell and machine-gun fire, led his two tanks to the lock under direct observation from the enemy.

Through his action he was instrumental in causing the machine-gunners to surrender and enabled the infantry to gain the eastern bank of the Sambre Canal.

Historically the action, of which the above was a small part, is generally regarded as being the last British tank operation of the First World War.

BELOW A Mark IV supply tank being guided through the ruins of Domart in September 1919. Notice that in this case it is armed with a Hotchkiss machine gun.

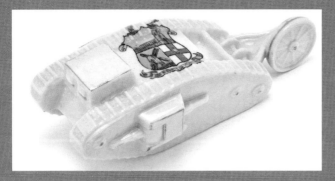

ABOVE China tank Mark I – one wheel has been portrayed at the rear of the tank as this was all that could be seen by the modellers who had only the *Daily Mirror* photographs of *Crème De Menthe* to study.

ABOVE A trench art model of a tank called *Nelson* made from shell driving barrels and brass shell cases. The brass plaque in front of the tank says '14 World War 18'. The maker was 96985 C.G.R. Fitch of the Tank Corps, who was invalided out of the Army in 1919, suffering from the effects of gas.

RIGHT A tank money box made out of wood from a crashed aircraft by Private Adams.

TANK SOUVENIRS – David Willey

Although the tank had a hesitant start on the battlefield and took over a year to make any significant impact, as a propaganda weapon it was an instant and popular success. The British press reported the use of the new 'heavy armoured car' or 'tank' only days after its first use on 15 September 1916. However, it was not until 22 November that the *Daily Mirror* published the first photograph of a tank (having paid a sizeable sum to a charity for the privilege). In the meantime cartoonists and artists had a field day imagining what a tank would look like. The images of C5, *Crème de Menthe*, that the *Daily Mirror* published were confusing, as this Mark I tank had one of the wheels at the rear blown off before advancing into action on 15 September. The image was all that the souvenir manufacturers initially had to go on and so the first model china commemorative tank was reproduced with only one wheel.

Despite the popularity of the tank with the public (it was seen by millions for the first time on film in *The Battle of the Ancre and the Advance of the Tanks* in January 1917) the various souvenir items made to celebrate this new British weapon were often far from

THE DAILY MIRROR, Wednesday, November 22, 1916.

FIRST PICTURES OF THE TANKS IN ACTION

The Daily Mirror

CERTIFIED CIRCULATION LARGER THAN THAT OF ANY OTHER DAILY PICTURE PAPER

No. 4,082. Registered at the G.P.O. as a Newspaper. WEDNESDAY, NOVEMBER 22, 1916. One Halfpenny.

"HUSH, HUSH"—A TANK GOES "GALUMPHANT" INTO ACTION ON THE WESTERN FRONT.

LEFT The Mark I, *Crème De Menthe*, as it first appeared to the British public on the cover of the *Daily Mirror* newspaper. The paper paid £1,000 to a charity for the rights to publish the photograph.

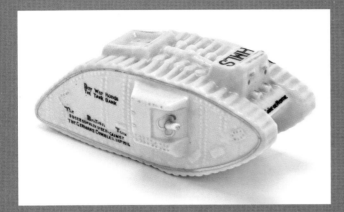

ABOVE Carlton Ware china Mark IV. The text on the side of the tank reads *'Buy War Bonds. The Tank Bank. The British Tank used successfully against the Germans, Combles Sep 1916.'*

ABOVE A cast iron money box or 'tank bank'. '119' was *Old Bill*, one of the tanks that toured Britain in 1918 as part of the War Bonds fundraising campaign.

accurate representations. The tank was British, it was a first (the other new wartime inventions had so far all come from the Germans, such as poison gas and Zeppelins) and it was instantly recognisable with its distinctive rhomboid shape. The tank therefore became *the* item to reproduce. Barbara Jones and Bill Howell state in their book *Popular Arts of the First World War* (Studio Vista, 1972) that in hand-made souvenirs and crested China 'there are more representing tanks than any other weapon or image of war'.

LEFT Tank Week lapel flag from the War Bonds fundraising effort in Bristol.

Crested china models, toys, inkwells, cigarette and jewellery boxes, teapots, whistles and lighters were all made in the shape of tanks. With the success of raising War Bonds with real tanks touring the country there came cast-iron 'tank banks' into which you could slot your pennies.

Trench art – items made from battlefield debris and military material by soldiers – also includes an amazing number of tank portrayals. The tricky issue of tracks was approached in a number of ways. One of the cleverest was the use of the brass driving bands from fired shells to reproduce the regular pattern of a track. Some soldiers made beautifully detailed models of tanks – perhaps their 'bus' or vehicles they worked on. A number of these souvenir and trench art representations can be seen in the collections at the Tank Museum, some of which are reproduced here.

RIGHT Souvenir Tank Bank paper napkin.

Chapter Two

Anatomy of the Mark IV tank

Tanks were quite complex creations, even from the beginning. The method of construction was fairly straightforward, as were the mechanical components, but taken together they amounted to a complicated combination. Tracks in particular were an entirely original design. The fact that the tank was required to move across country, over ground that was almost impassable, was a measure of the mechanical complexity of the design.

OPPOSITE An internal view of the crew compartment showing the Daimler engine.

General description

In profile the tank was more or less a rhomboid, higher at the front than the back, and the outline of the track frames dominated the design. These were covered in panels of armour plate, all of riveted construction which was typical of the time. A raised cab at the front marked the location of the driver and commander, who observed the way ahead through hinged flaps that could be closed when the tank was under fire.

Weapons were carried in sponsons about midway along each side. The larger sponsons seen on male tanks each housed a 57mm, six-pounder gun while, while those on female tanks that were armed with machine guns only were much smaller. Each sponson, male or female, marked the location of two more crew members.

Inside the tank, in a more or less central position, was the six-cylinder Daimler engine, which drove through a primary gearbox and differential to secondary gearboxes in the frames at each side. Each of these was the station for another crew member, bringing the total complement up to eight. Drive then passed by a loop of chain in the frames on each side to a toothed drive sprocket at the back, which engaged with the inner face of the tracks. These tracks ran all the way around the track frames, giving the tank its excellent cross-country performance. A 70-gallon fuel tank was situated low down at the back.

The hull

The most significant part of the hull was the track frames on each side. These bore all the weight and gave the tank its structural strength. Each frame comprised an inner and outer structure about 22in apart, made stronger by internal cross pieces. Externally they consisted of panels of armour plate riveted to un-armoured girders.

The rest of the tank, between the frames, consisted of a rear panel, roof, front cab and pointed nose, and of course a floor. These were all attached by rivets except the roof, which was bolted in place to enable the engine to be lifted out for major repair or replacement. The rear plate was a two-piece item with openings for a small rear door and a ventilator, while the roof, which consisted of a series of panels, had openings for the engine exhaust pipes and an upper hatch. Ahead of the roof was the cab, which had hinged panels in the front face to enable the crew to see out. Below the cab at the very front were two sloped panels that met at the nose that provided leg room for the crew. The floor, which was also composed of individual panels, was more thinly armoured than the rest of the tank since it was rarely exposed.

Sponsons were provided on each side to carry the guns – 57mm cannon in the larger male sponsons, and two Lewis machine guns in the much smaller female sponsons. These were also of riveted construction and designed to fold inwards for rail travel.

Daimler 105hp engine

Many people express surprise on learning that the engine in the Mark IV tank is a Daimler, believing it to be a German type. In fact an independent company, authorised to use Daimler patents, had been established in Britain in 1891 and by 1896 had set up in a factory in Coventry as the Daimler Motor Company, an entirely British concern. The prime mover in this acquisition was the engineer Frederick R. Simms, whose name is still associated with automotive components, but things got off to a shaky start when Simms became associated with the entrepreneur Harry J. Lawson. Lawson made, and then lost, a fortune buying up patents relating to motor vehicles and founded what he called the Great Horseless Carriage Company. He also purchased the building in Coventry, known as the Motor Mills, which shared the site with the Daimler factory, and Lawson himself remained closely involved with Simms and the company for some time so for a while its future was in some doubt.

Under prudent management the firm survived, aided by some welcome royal patronage, and in 1906 they adopted the sleeve-valve system invented by the American Charles Yale Knight. Charles Knight, a native of Wisconsin, was not exactly a qualified engineer, but having dedicated himself to producing a silent, or near silent motor-car engine employing sleeve valves instead of the noisy poppet valves he eventually succeeded, producing what was marketed as the Silent Knight engine. Knight came to Britain around 1907 and clearly impressed the people at Daimler with his design, although they felt that the standard of engineering could be improved upon. By 1908 the British firm had an engine they could be proud of, and it is said that production of Daimler poppet-valve engines ended virtually overnight. At this time Daimler was known primarily as a manufacturer of high-quality automobiles, although they had tried their hand with a limited number of light commercials, and the management was keen that they should become involved in this market. To begin with they appear to have built mostly prototypes and trials vehicles but in due course they settled down to develop a range of conventional lorries and buses, production of which expanded dramatically as the threat of war drew closer.

The Daimler Motor Company was also anxious to get involved in the agricultural market. Although at this time steam dominated this area, internal combustion tractors were starting to make inroads, particularly among enlightened companies like William Foster & Co. of Lincoln under their new managing director William Tritton. The first Daimler farm tractor, a gawky-looking thing like a child's idea of a steam engine, appeared in 1911, apparently designed in conjunction with Foster's, but the real breakthrough came when Tritton visited South America shortly before the war and came home with a substantial quantity of orders for internal combustion tractors. In the pampas regions in particular, coal and even wood was not that easy to come by, and while some British engine builders had developed straw-burning steam engines, these were voracious consumers and liquid fuel was regarded as the ideal solution.

So working in conjunction with Daimler Foster's produced a range of tractors for export, the largest of which was powered by a new 105hp, six-cylinder engine employing the Knight sleeve-valve system. It is also worth

BELOW Foster's Centipede tractor of 1913. Essentially a half-track, as it would be described today, although the tracks proved to be more trouble than Tritton thought they were worth.

British Mark IV tank.

(Ian Moores/www.ianmooresgraphics.com)

1 Track tensioning adjuster
2 Commander's seat
3 Daimler 105hp engine
4 Port side male sponson
5 Six-pounder gun, port side
6 Lewis machine gun
7 Starting handle
8 Secondary gears, port side
9 Differential housing
10 Drive sprocket, port side
11 Roof stowage tray
12 Rear hatch and lookout
13 Exhaust silencer
14 Exhaust stack
15 Ammunition stowage
16 Un-ditching beam rails
17 Driver's vision port
18 Front Lewis machine gun
19 Steering brake levers
20 Front towing eye and bracket
21 Final drive chain, port side
22 Driver's seat
23 Periscope aperture cover
24 Clutch lever
25 Pistol port
26 Starting crank engagement point
27 Vision slit
28 Floor boards
29 Starboard side male sponson
30 Exhaust pipe

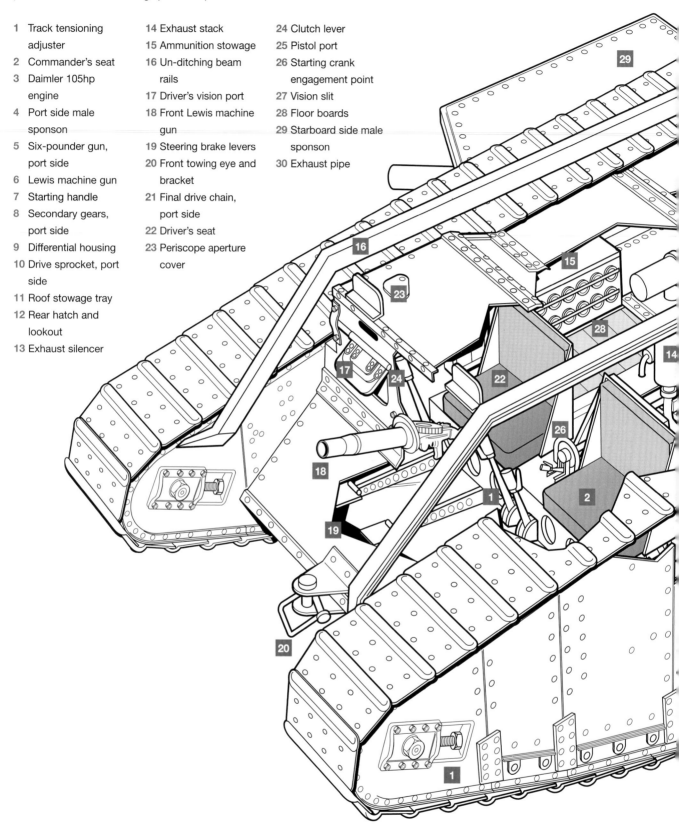

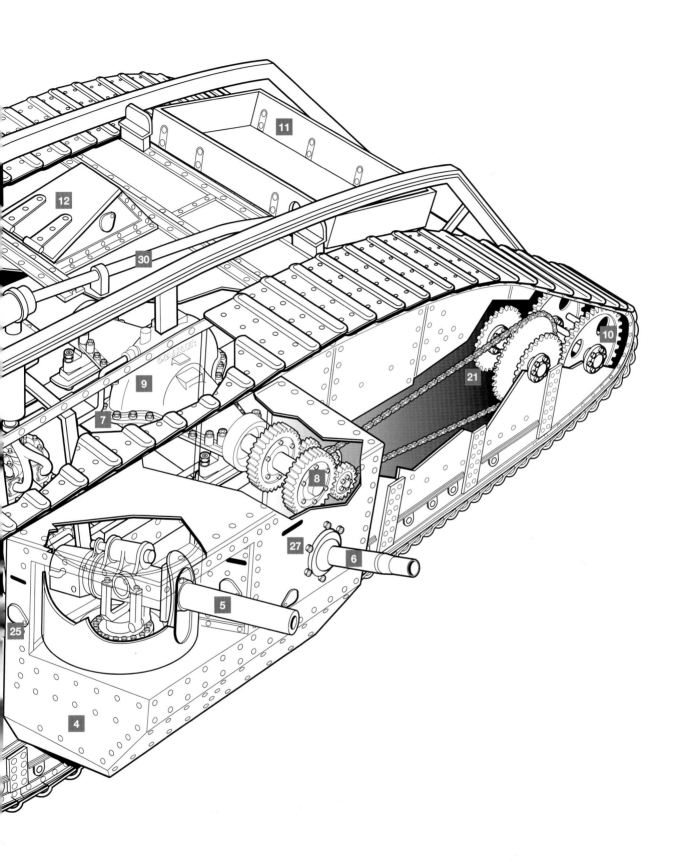

noting that in 1913 Foster's built a track-laying tractor called the Centipede for a customer in Paraguay, but the experience of operating it, on trials, almost put William Tritton off the idea of crawler tracks for life.

The 105hp engine was incorporated into a massive wheeled tractor designed by Foster's for the Admiralty and usually known as the Foster-Daimler tractor. To look at, it resembled a steam traction engine but without the firebox and boiler. Instead power was provided by a 105hp petrol engine driving through a cone clutch and gearbox (giving two speeds forward and one in reverse) into an enormous worm drive differential at the back. It was this combination, known at least to Foster's as the Daimler set, that provided the power for most British tanks up to and including the Mark IV. The engine was mechanically governed at 1,000rpm, which was quite slow even for a petrol engine of those days, and it rotated in a clockwise direction, viewed from the rear.

The large Daimler engine was quite unusual

for its day. Most big internal combustion engined tractors of that time used massive paraffin or heavy oil engines. However, the combination of Daimler's high-quality engineering and Knight's double sleeve-valve system produced a reliable and relatively silent power unit. It had a cubic capacity of 13 litres comprising six cylinders each 150mm x 150mm, what is sometimes referred to as a square engine. The cylinder heads were cast in pairs but the body of the block and the sump were in aluminium. Knight's sleeve-valve system employed two concentric sleeves, between the piston and the cylinder liner, which moved vertically to open and close the inlet and exhaust ports as required. The sleeves were driven from a half-time shaft that derived power from the crankshaft, in much the same way as a conventional camshaft does. The advantages of the sleeve-valve system were that it needed less adjustment, suffered less from carbon build-up in the valve ports, and was relatively quiet, at least compared with poppet valves as

BELOW A Foster-Daimler tractor posed at the works with the engine just visible below the big fuel tank. Notice how the sump hangs down below chassis level.

they were at that time. It was also said to be an excellent system for larger engines developing maximum torque at low revs. The main disadvantage was that the sleeves were difficult to lubricate, at least until Daimler introduced a system of perforations and grooves both to spread and retain the lubricant. On the inlet side of the engine, that is to say the right side looking forward, there was a Zenith 48mm carburettor, linked to the engine governor, and a type KW magneto.

An oil tank, located above and behind the engine, supplied oil to a pump which in turn filled a series of troughs in the sump, beneath the connecting rods. These dipped into the oil as they rotated and splashed oil up into the other working parts while the engine was running. Oil then trickled down into the sump where it was picked up by another pump and sent back to the engine oil tank. For this reason crews were instructed only to top up the engine oil tank when the engine was running. Otherwise the action of the pump in the sump could result in too much oil entering the oil tank, which could then overflow. Both pumps were also provided with additional pipes that delivered oil to other parts of the engine. Smaller fittings such as the magneto and governor had to be oiled more carefully so this was a separate crew duty.

The engine was water-cooled with a water jacket encasing each pair of cylinders and an impeller pump to maintain circulation, located on the exhaust side of the engine. Some early Mark IV tanks, perhaps some of the first male machines built by Foster's of Lincoln for example, were fitted with the large, box-shaped envelope radiator that was found in the Mark I tanks and other early models, but this was soon replaced in the Mark IV – but only the Mark IV – by a pair of smaller, slimmer tubular radiators of a more conventional pattern. An expert with a trained eye can distinguish between the two from the outside at the back because they had different filling and draining points, although this requires skilled and careful scrutiny because

BELOW A Daimler set, engine, gearbox and differential on a subframe ready to be installed in a tank. Mounted at the rear is a tubular radiator.

ABOVE **A photograph of tanks under construction at Beardmore's works in Glasgow, showing the installation of the tubular radiator at the rear of the tank.**

older-pattern radiators were replaced by the newer type during a tank's life, resulting in modifications to the original layout that are not always easy to detect.

Those at the Tank Corps' Central Workshops in France were not entirely satisfied with either design. The original envelope radiator was in the form of a large, rectangular box containing 40 big envelopes made from copper sheet. These were connected to one another by a series of aluminium rings, with rubber washers sandwiched between them so that hot water, entering at the top, trickled down through the various envelopes to the bottom. A large fan in a casing alongside the radiator, driven by a segmented leather belt from the engine, sent colder air between the envelopes to assist in the cooling process so that the water, by the time it reached the lower pipe that carried it back to the engine, was suitably moderated in temperature. Central Workshops found that as time went by sections of these copper envelopes developed bulges that constricted air flow so they had to be replaced. However, it is worth recording that Central Workshops' own records show that they repaired 97 envelope radiators in the year ending 31 December 1918, which is some indication of how many early tanks were still in service.

Clearly there were great hopes that the new, tubular radiators would not only prove more efficient but also less troublesome, although in this respect Central Workshops were to

be disappointed. For example, it was soon discovered that leaking of coolant water was becoming endemic and investigation by the staff at Central Workshops revealed that the vertical tubes, which provided the cooling element of the radiator, had been fitted with rubber rings at each end where they connected with the upper and lower plates. The object seems to have been to allow for expansion but, due to the poor quality of the rubber, the rings soon perished and caused leaks. Following a period of experimentation Central Workshops came up with a solution involving the use of lead and cork instead of rubber. Once this fault was identified the engineers in France reported back to the authorities in Britain requesting that the method of assembling radiators be changed, although Lieutenant Colonel Brockbank, DSO, commanding Central Workshops, who compiled the report at the end of the war wrote that even then new radiators were being delivered from Britain with the rubber rings, which had to be replaced the first time they failed.

Incidentally, cooling air, which the fan blew through the radiator, was drawn directly from inside the tank. This, in theory, should have kept the crew area free from toxic fumes and reduced the heat, but in fact the capacity of the Daimler engine to produce both was such as to overcome this effect. And it was this movement of air that reversed the normal cooling flow of the Lewis gun, drawing fumes directly into the gunner's face and making his job more difficult.

Although anti-freeze as we understand it was not available then, a proportion of glycerine in the coolant water was known to prevent water from freezing in the winter. All the same the staff at Central Workshops did not like it; they claimed that it could clog water pipes and ruined rubber joints in the cooling system. They advocated draining down the system overnight, although this was not the straightforward task that it ought to have been. For the radiator itself it was no problem, a tap near the base emptied it completely, but there were other parts of the system where it was not so easy, in particular the cylinder heads. These had to be emptied entirely; otherwise if the water froze the damage could be serious. To this end the crew were provided with a syringe that could be used to remove residual water from each cylinder-head jacket once a brass bolt was removed. If, having done this, any water remained, the handbook required that the fan drive belt be detached and the engine run for up to 20 minutes every 2 or 3 hours.

Gears and gearboxes

From the engine, crankshaft drive passed into a large flywheel that contained what is described as the female part of the cone clutch; it was always turning when the engine was running but had no fore and aft movement. That was left to the male cone, which slid forwards into the female cone by the action of the clutch pedal and lever.

The clutch pedal, which unlike modern practice was activated by the driver's right foot, also had a lever attached within reach of the driver's right hand. Since the action of the clutch required considerable strength this enabled the driver to give his foot a rest during a long trek that might involve constant stopping and starting.

The male portion of the cone clutch was surfaced with a heat-resistant material such as Ferodo, held in place by rivets. A good deal of heat could be generated when the clutch was engaged so some sort of heat-proof lining obviated this. When the clutch was disengaged

the male portion of the cone was withdrawn and came into contact with two clutch stops, also lined with Ferodo, which acted like brakes to slow down the gears in the final drive, otherwise changing gear became impossible.

The primary gearbox was located towards the rear of the tank, behind the engine, and attached directly to the lower section of the differential casing. However, it was activated by a gated lever, to the left of the driver, which was connected to the gearbox by pushrods. This gearbox provided two forward speeds and one reverse with the respective ratios of 1:1, 1:1.75

ABOVE Gearbox, clutch and differential photographed during the restoration of tank 2324.

FAR LEFT F4, *Flirt II*, attacking a steep bank at Wailly. At times like this one hopes that all the loose items stowed on top do not fall off.

LEFT F4, *Flirt II*, about to take the plunge. Naturally, in all these manoeuvres very careful driving was required. Many trainee drivers found the drop the most frightening manoeuvre of all.

and in reverse 1:1.4. Not a lot in it, but sufficient when used in conjunction with the secondary gears, to translate the torque delivered by the engine into remarkable climbing power. Typical of heavy vehicles of that time the gears were square cut so that changing on the move was virtually impossible, even with the time-honoured practice of double declutching.

Directly behind the gearbox and attached to it was the differential, housed inside a massive casting that dominated the rear end of the tank. Drive from the gearbox terminated in a steel worm that meshed with a large-diameter bronze worm wheel and that in turn activated a nest of bevel gears which imparted the differential action to a pair of half-shafts that, in a conventional vehicle, constituted the rear axle. The function of the differential in the Mark IV tank, as indeed it was on most motorised vehicles, was to divide the drive to each side so that the vehicle could turn left or right. Without it the vehicle would only ever be able to proceed in a straight line.

Of course there were times when differential action was not desirable – when steering on the secondary gears for instance – so when necessary the driver could activate a differential lock, using a lever attached to the roof of the tank above his left shoulder. Drivers were instructed to lock the differential when tackling

a steep slope, either up or down, or when using the undilching beam, for example.

Lubrication was required on all the features mentioned so far. On the clutch of course this had to be done with care since lubricant, or indeed water, on the surfaces of the cone would render the clutch inoperative. The gearbox itself contained gear oil up to a certain level, which had to be maintained while the differential contained some oil in the differential case, although the white-metal bearings in which the main worm wheel ran were lubricated by wicks that received oil from a small container on the differential casing.

Drive from the differential and the half-shafts leading from it now passed into two-speed secondary gears in the track frames on either side of the tank. Levers, accessible in the frames, enabled a secondary gearsman to select one or other of these gears on instructions from the driver. A toggle arrangement built into the system prevented both gears from being engaged at once. However, unless these gears were employed, drive to the tracks would be incomplete and the tank would go nowhere. Thus it was impossible to drive the tank on the primary gearbox alone. Secondary gears had been included in the drive train to provide more flexibility in a 28-ton tank. By selecting the ideal

RIGHT The secondary gear levers on the starboard side. The primary gearbox is located under the wooden platform on the right. Notice, too, that the Daimler engine is covered over, which at least protected the crew to some extent. The bulge on the side enclosed the engine governor.

combination of primary and secondary gears the driver now had an option of four forward speeds and two reverse, which could be important when selecting the ideal gears to suit the ground ahead of the tank.

These secondary gears also had a part to play in steering the tank, as explained elsewhere, and naturally they had to be engaged to give effect to the track brakes. If a track was out of gear then the track brakes were useless. The driver's handbook describes these brakes – operated by levers worked from the seat to the left of the driver – as band brakes, lined with Ferodo and acting in a brake drum on each side. Their main function was in connection with steering and the handbook warns that for this reason they tended to wear out rather fast and require constant adjustment. Driving the Tank Museum's Mark IV these authors found them to be virtually useless.

ABOVE A Mark IV training tank demonstrates its trench-crossing ability before an invited audience. The driver has to approach the trench square on and keep moving.

LEFT Drivers were advised not to try and take a trench obliquely, otherwise this might happen.

ABOVE A delivery of
fuel is unloaded from
the back of a three-
ton lorry. It was fed
direct into the tank
by hand from these
cans, and extra cans
were stowed on and in
the tank. Most of the
tanks in the picture are
Mark IV, although the
one without sponsons
in the foreground is a
Mark I.

RIGHT The fuel tank
on the Mark IV was
located outside at the
back. It had a total
capacity of 70gal,
which was sufficient
to run the tank for 35
miles on good going.

FAR RIGHT The
fuel filler cap was
in the centre at the
top, underneath an
armoured flap that is
missing in this picture.

Petrol and petrol supply

The fuel supplied for tanks in 1916 and 1917 was reckoned to be of the poorest quality available. In the trade it seems to have been referred to as US Navy gasoline with a rating of about 45 octane. In the British services the highest grade of fuel was reserved for aircraft, the middling grades for staff cars and transport, while the lower grades were considered suitable for tractors, heavy transport vehicles and tanks which, on account of their slow speed and ponderous progress, were only considered

worthy of the lowest grade of all. Whether this would have made much difference in the case of the stolid old Daimler engine is difficult to say but investigations carried out by Harry Ricardo and his team, assisted by Sir Robert Waley Cohen of Shell, first drew attention to this fact. Ricardo was anxious to find a better-quality fuel for his new 150hp engine.

The Mark IV had a 70gal fuel tank between the rear horns, low down at the back and protected by an armour-plate box. On reasonable going this gave the tank the ability to travel 35 miles before refuelling, although it is unlikely that the crew would permit the fuel level to drop that low if they could help it. Impurities in the fuel itself along with the risk of contamination by dirt from outside could soon clog up the petrol feed system and bring the tank to a halt. Official publications on the operation and maintenance of the Mark IV drive home the message of cleanliness, with repeated

reminders, and the crew are enjoined to strip and clean all filters and sumps on a daily basis in hopes of avoiding this.

Since the new fuel tank was lower than the carburettor it was necessary to pressurise the system. On earlier tanks the total fuel capacity was 50gal, held in two 25gal tanks high up to the front, which supplied fuel to the carburettor by gravity. However, the fire risk was high and in any case more capacity was needed to give the tank a longer range, so in the Mark IV fuel was carried in a relocated 70gal container. To begin with an air-pressure system was installed. To build up the necessary pressure before starting, the driver operated a hand pump situated near his left leg, attached to the front seat support. This pump was pivoted and in order to operate it the driver swung the pump over to the left, closed the pressure release cock connected to it and pumped until the pressure gauge, also attached, registered at least 2lb. He then swung the pump to the right, which sealed the air system and prevented leakage, and once this was done he turned on the petrol stop cock.

Once the engine was running air pressure was maintained by a mechanical pump located on the induction (right) side of the engine below the second cylinder. This pumped air through a pipe running along the roof of the vehicle and down into the fuel tank. Another pipe linked the fuel tank with the carburettor. Air pressure constantly bore down upon the fuel, which was then forced up the pipe to the carburettor.

The problem with this was simply maintaining pressure. Air leaks could develop in the pipe itself, at joints or indeed in the actual petrol tank, and once that happened the entire system broke down. As a result a more reliable system, known as the Autovac, was introduced. As its name implies this relied on creating a vacuum to move the fuel and it was manufactured by the Autovac Manufacturing Co. Ltd of Stockport who marketed it for use in cars of the period.

In a Mark IV tank the Autovac was installed about halfway along the engine, attached to the roof and linked to the carburettor and engine-driven air pump, the hand pump by the driver's seat having been disconnected and removed. A reserve of fuel was retained in the bottom half of the Autovac, suspended above which was a float. The action of the air pump created a partial

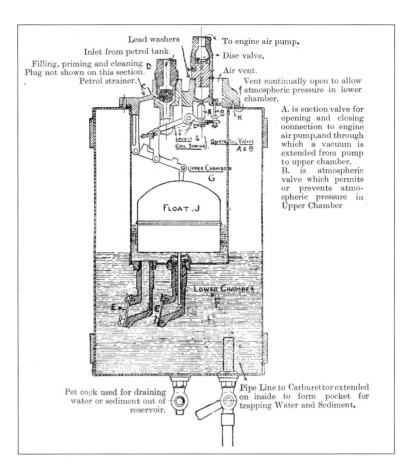

ABOVE The fuel delivery system relied on a patented device known as an Autovac, the workings of which are shown in this diagram taken from the Mark IV crew handbook.

BELOW The Mark IV female tank, *Grit*, at the Australian War Memorial in Canberra seems to be the only one still with its Autovac in place.

vacuum in the upper chamber of the Autovac that could only be cured by fuel drawn from the main petrol tank. This caused the float to rise, closing off the suction valve and opening an atmospheric pressure valve which shut off fuel from the main tank and drained down the petrol held in the Autovac to the carburettor as required. This procedure was repeated continuously.

Like any other fuel system of that time the Autovac was susceptible to dirt and air leaks, remedies for which were laid out in the official publications, but it must have been considered reasonably effective since it was employed in all subsequent British tanks up to the end of the First World War

Tracks, spuds and unditching beams

Most people who study the origins of the British tank are likely to agree that the one feature that ensured the ultimate success of the design had to be the tracks. Sir Albert Stern certainly thought so. Writing in 1919 (*Log-Book of a Pioneer*) he first quoted the famous telegram that landed on his desk on 22 September 1915: 'Balata died on test bench yesterday morning. New arrival by Tritton out of Pressed Plate. Light in weight but very strong. All doing well, thank you.

Proud Parents.'

Stern said, 'This was the birth of the Tank.' And he was quite right. The new track designed by Sir William Tritton and first applied to *Little Willie* late in 1915 was virtually identical to the type fitted to most British tanks for the duration of the war. But it was this that enabled his colleague Walter Wilson the freedom to adopt the all-round track configuration that was the

hallmark of the British heavy tank of the First World War.

Each link consisted of a sole plate of armoured steel 6mm thick and measuring 20½in by 7½in, flat but with a raised lip, or spud, at the leading edge to provide grip. (The use of metric measurements for armour thickness and imperial for the dimensions of the item was normal practice concerning tanks in the First World War.) Riveted to each sole plate were two stamped, or later drop forged, links, a matching but opposed pair that fulfilled a variety of functions. First, they were connected to an adjacent pair on the next sole plate and joined by 1in pins that acted as hinges between that track link and its neighbours. Second, the smooth inner surfaces of the links formed a pathway upon which the track rollers ran. Third, the extreme outer edges of this flat surface engaged with rails on both inner faces of the track frames and were thus unable to drop away from the frames when unsupported, reducing the risk of a tank running off its tracks. Finally, slots between the flat surfaces of each link acted as a receptacle for the individual teeth of the twin-track driving sprockets as they turned and propelled the tank itself along its tracks. An official crew handbook instructed crews to ensure that these slots are kept free of mud which, if it baked hard might cause the tracks to ride over the teeth of the sprockets, rather than mesh with them and either break or come off.

There is a distinct difference between the way in which a tank, or any other tracked vehicle, moves across the ground compared with a wheeled vehicle such as a bicycle, car or bus for instance, but it is not always obvious. Wheeled vehicles move by direct interaction with the ground surface whereas

BELOW A drawing of a track plate showing the raised lip and the rivet pattern.

BELOW RIGHT Drawings of a track link; these were riveted in pairs to the inner surface of the track plate.

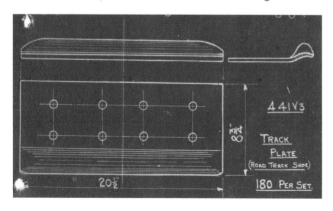

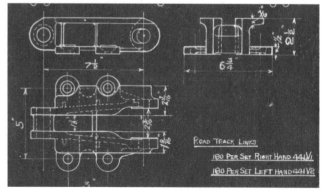

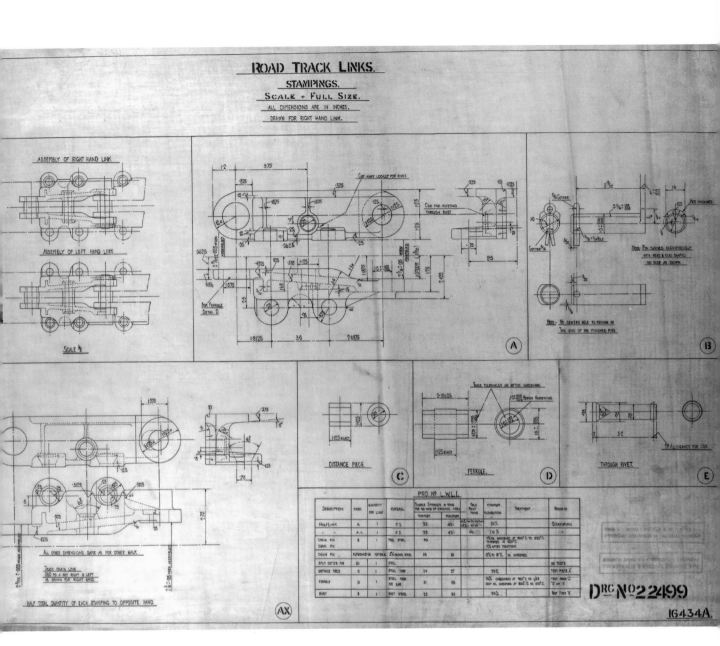

ROAD TRACK LINKS.

STAMPINGS.

SCALE + FULL SIZE.

ALL DIMENSIONS ARE IN INCHES.

DRAWN FOR RIGHT HAND LINK.

ASSEMBLY OF RIGHT HAND LINK.

ASSEMBLY OF LEFT HAND LINK.

SCALE ½

DISTANCE PIECE (C)

FERRULE. (D)

THROUGH RIVET. (E)

DRG Nº 22499

16434A.

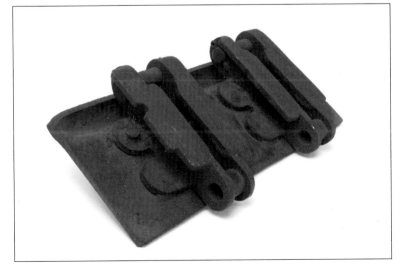

ABOVE The original Mark IV drawings for the linking section of a track plate.

LEFT A complete track link from a Mark IV showing the plate, in contact with the ground and the links riveted to it. Note in particular the flange on the outer edge of each link that held the lower run of the track in place.

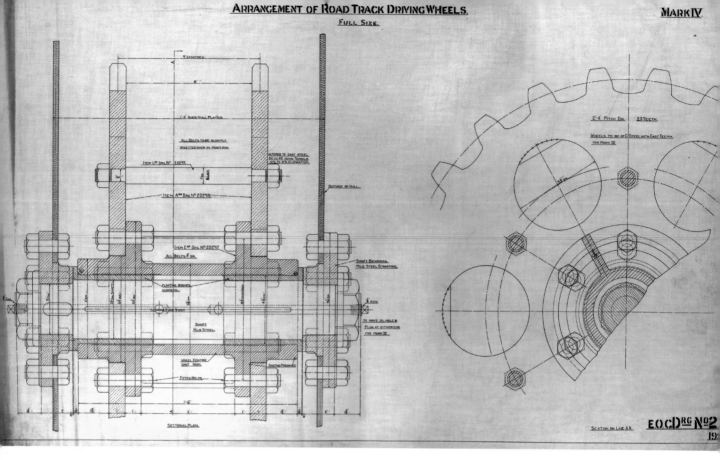

EOCD^{RG} N°2

SECTIONAL PLAN.

SECTION ON LINE A.A.

ABOVE Sectional drawings of road track driving wheels for the Mark IV.

tracked vehicles do not. In this case it is the track that provides the surface for the vehicle to move along and is probably best described by the 19th-century term 'portable railway'. In other words the vehicle lays the track upon the ground in front of itself, crawls along it and then lifts it up at the other end and carries it forwards again. This is just as true in the case of a modern tracked vehicle as it was in 1917, although it is not so easy to detect.

Drive to the tracks on either side began on countershafts parallel to the secondary gear shafts within the track frames. These countershafts carried two sprockets that meshed with those on the primary shafts, depending upon which gear was selected, and a sturdy sprocket in the centre engaged with a loop of chain that carried the drive on. This chain, known in the trade as bush roller chain, was a heavy-duty version of a product patented by Hans Renold of Manchester, but in this case manufactured and supplied by their rivals the Coventry Chain Company. This loop of chain, essentially like a large bicycle chain, carried the drive back to another sprocket with gears on the same shaft, either side of the central chain sprocket, which meshed directly with the teeth of the track drive sprockets on each side.

The drive sprockets were probably the key item in the entire make-up of the Mark IV tank, indeed as it was in most tanks. Each sprocket consisted of a pair of toothed discs, 27in in diameter and spaced to engage with slots in the inner face of each track link. Thus it was the sprockets, deriving their power indirectly from the engine, that pulled the tank along its tracks. As a result the teeth on the sprockets soon wore out, probably not helped by the fact that those same teeth engaged with gears on the adjacent shaft. The demand for replacement sprockets, therefore, far outstripped availability since the delivery of spare parts from Britain was far in arrears, even of such vital components. Consequently Central Workshops in France attempted to get sprockets cut locally but found it almost impossible to persuade any of the local French engineering firms to undertake the task. In the end, only by ignoring strict instructions from Britain and revealing to one firm that these items were required for tanks, were they able to get replacement sprockets made. Central Workshops claimed that the French items were not as well made as those produced in Britain, but since they worked and in any case were all that could be obtained, they were used until the situation remedied itself.

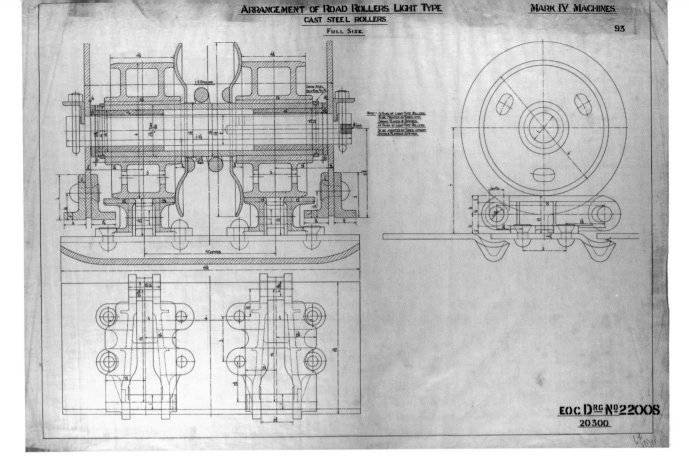

EOC. DRG No 2200S

20300

One thing many people do not realise is that the underside of the track frames on a typical First World War tank are not flat, but gently curved. There is a reason for this although it is not immediately obvious. If you examine a Mark IV tank standing on a hard surface you will notice that, at most, ten track plates per side are in contact with the ground. This is done to make steering – or swinging, to use the word of the time – that much easier. The shorter the track actually in touch with the ground the less lateral resistance there is to the slewing motion that swings the tank on to a new heading. Conversely, on softer ground the tank sinks in so that more track links are in contact with the surface, which reduces the ground pressure exerted by the tank but it means that turning becomes that bit more difficult. Of course there comes a point, as Douglas Browne discovered in the slushy conditions at Third Ypres, when the tank sinks so deep that steering is virtually impossible and all one can do is plough straight ahead until water seeps inside the tank, works its way into the clutch and brings the vehicle to a halt.

However, that is an extreme case and under normal circumstances, over typical country, the tank makes its way with only modest sinkage. Even so, as already explained, it is the tank, dragging itself along the tracks, which is actually making progress and not the tracks themselves, as it seems. Consequently, in addition to the drive sprockets, the tank is carried along the tracks by a series of rollers, held on short shafts within the frames of the tank. As usual even this is not a simple matter. There are in fact four types of roller: light flanged rollers; light plain rollers; heavy flanged rollers; and heavy plain rollers. The heavy rollers are situated centrally on each side because they take the greatest weight, with the light rollers at both ends acting as load carriers when the tank is climbing or descending a steep slope.

The plain rollers, of which there are 15 on each side, are simply load carriers, while the flanged rollers, as their name implies, are flanged like railway wheels and besides taking the weight help to keep the tank on its tracks as it moves along. It is also worth noting that the flanged rollers, and only the flanged rollers on each shaft, are separated by a spring that keeps the flanges pressed against the inside edges of the track links. These springs do not do anything else; they could not in any way be described as part of a suspension system.

ABOVE Arrangement of light type rollers for the Mark IV.

RIGHT Adjusting track for the correct tension was done at the front, using the threaded bolt shown here to move the track idler wheel.

The fact that the track links themselves are flanged and held in place within the frames has already been mentioned, but this only applies to the lower run of the track on each side. These flanges are engaged by what were known as switch plates at the front and then are released close to the rear of the tank.

It seems hard to imagine but tank tracks stretch; very slowly it is true but over time, if not corrected, it can become serious. Track links fail to match up with drive sprocket teeth and, if the tracks get slack enough they can come off. The initial remedy is to adjust the tension of the track by adjusting the idler wheels on each side at the front. The idler wheel on the Mark IV is at the very front of the track frames in a section normally referred to as the horns. It is from the idlers that the tracks pass down to ground level and provide a pathway for the tank to drive over until they are picked up by the drive sprocket at the back. Thus the idler serves two purposes:

to begin with it keeps the track on its path and serves as a means of supporting the tracks when approaching an obstacle, like the parapet of a trench for example. Second, the idlers can be adjusted, within limits, to take up any slack that might have developed in the track.

First two large nuts holding the idler shaft in place have to be slackened off and then the crew members use a spanner on a large bolt, which effectively shifts the idler forward until the track is judged to be at the correct tension. The method of doing this, as described in the tank driver's handbook, has a certain unscientific practicality about it. Apparently the trick is to insert a large spanner, or better still a crowbar, beneath the track where it slopes down at the rear of the tank, and work it up and down; if the track moves about one inch, then tension is correct. In the event that track becomes too slack to adjust by this method it would be necessary to remove a whole link – this would have been quite drastic on a tank in the First World War, probably indicating that it was time the entire set of tracks were replaced.

After passing around the drive sprockets at the back, the tracks proceed along the top of the tank over steel rails, bronze blocks and one set of flanged rollers per side until they reach the front and travel around the idlers again.

Although it tended to attract mud and grit the tracks were lubricated. Two containers, with screw-top caps, were located underneath the bench seat at the front of the tank. One container served each track and was filled with thick oil that was delivered by gravity drip feed down pipes through the frames to the track. This oil was then carried around to lubricate the top run of the tracks which, on earlier models, were fed with grease from a grease gun. The grease gun was also used to lubricate the spindles of the track rollers and the spindles of the idler.

Douglas Browne, in *The Tank in Action*, records that during the night of 30 July 1917 he and his crew spent the last hour before moving off fitting spuds to the tracks of his tank, G46. These spuds, or iron shoes as he refers to them elsewhere, were in effect an adjustable extension that could be clamped to a track link providing extra surface contact, and a sort of blade which gave the tank additional grip on a

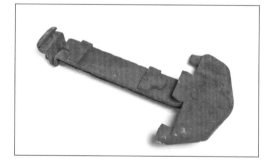

RIGHT A track spud, or grouser, retrieved from a battlefield in France and photographed from both sides. The method of attaching it to a track link can be seen.

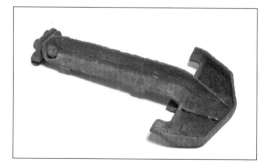

RIGHT Grouser spud, bottom view.

soft and slippery surface. Browne writes that this task could only be done at the last moment because these attachments did not work well on a hard surface; they could be crushed and bent by the weight of a tank and could even twist, or break, the track link to which they were fastened.

According to Browne he and his crew were required to fit 30 spuds to G46 but, due to the stiffness of nuts and bolts and a shortage of spanners, they only managed to fit about 15 in time and threw the rest into a ditch under the hedge at Frascati Farm, where the tanks had parked up earlier that day in preparation for what history now knows as the Battle of Third Ypres on the 31st. Browne notes that each tank carried 44 spuds in a box on the roof and complains that their weight, added to that of the unditching beam and its attachments, probably added about two tons to the overall weight of the tank.

Received opinion once had it that these spuds, fixed to every sixth track link were a characteristic feature of the Mark II tank, but examination of photographs shows that they were also fitted to some Mark I tanks – including at least one in Palestine – and many Mark IV tanks in 1917 and 1918, although not, as far as one can tell, to the Mark V or any other type. Some 30 spuds, fitted to 180 track links on a Mark IV tank equated to 15 each side attached to every 6th link. Browne indicates that this was not always adhered to and some very odd arrangements are seen; whether these were simply due to a job done in a hurry or the theory and fancy of a particular crew is not clear. Incidentally photographs of the Mark II male tank *Iron Duke* show it in Arras fitted with spuds. This suggests that damage suffered when driven on a solid road surface was only learned the hard way.

Another early device, a predecessor of the unditching beam was the torpedo spud, two of which were supplied to each tank. It consisted of a wooden spar, some 55in long by 6in in diameter, with iron collars at each end and a strong central collar linked by chains to a clamp that attached it to a track link. The idea was that with a torpedo spud fitted each side the spars would act as a purchase for the tracks if the tank became stuck. Browne felt they

had little to recommend them, explaining that in very muddy conditions the spar itself could turn sideways and be dragged the full length of the tank without putting up any resistance at all. According to the War Diary of Central Workshops, the torpedo spud design is credited to Major Harry Buddicom, who specialised in the design of unditching equipment.

The origins of the unditching beam device are described by Central Workshops as entirely accidental. They record that tanks, advancing to take part in the Battle of Arras in April 1917, and becoming bogged down in the mud, their crews cast about for a suitable means to get them out. Wooden sleepers from a ruined railway line in the vicinity were dragged across to the stranded tanks and attached to the tracks using the metal fittings from Buddicom's two torpedo spuds. Now, with a sleeper attached to both tracks the tanks managed to extricate themselves. Although at this time the tanks involved would not have been Mark IV machines, they nevertheless established the principle, and after further experimentation by Central Workshops a device was designed, based on the original idea. This involved a hefty beam of oak, roughly a trapezoid shape in section, with sheets of steel on two opposite sides and fittings derived from those on the spuds, by means of which the beam could be attached to the tracks.

Since the beam was too heavy to manhandle, Central Workshops devised a system of angle-iron rails, running the full length of the tank, upon which the beam was stowed when not in use. Since these rails cleared all the obstacles on top of the tank, from the spud box at the back, over the raised hatch and silencer to the cab at the front, it meant that the beam, once fastened to the tracks, could be drawn forwards without hindrance to drop

proposal and in the event the staff at Central Workshops were themselves saddled with the task of manufacturing and fitting all of the unditching gear for every Mark IV tank delivered to France, so that in theory any photograph of a Mark IV tank with unditching gear must indicate a tank that saw service in that country.

The practical effect of this unditching system should have been a great improvement, yet it was somewhat risky and had its limitations. For example, if the tank became stuck it required at least two members of the crew to leave the relative security of the tank and climb up on top, possibly under a hail of enemy fire. Granted this was no worse than in pre-unditching-beam days when other devices had to be employed or the area scoured for local materials, but the task facing these 'volunteers' was now a rather more cold-blooded affair.

down in front of the tank where it became a purchase for the tracks to bite on. If it worked and the tank freed itself the beam then reappeared at the back and was drawn up on to the rails by the continued movement of the tracks until it reached its stowed position. Once the system had been perfected at France's Central Workshops, reputedly by Major Philip Johnson of Number 3 Advanced Workshops, the drawings were submitted to Britain for production. Unfortunately industrial inertia and official red tape combined to defeat this

Even though the tank has now come to rest the tracks will still go around; however, with nothing but mud to bite on they simply thrash around and the tank itself is going nowhere. Two men now have to debus from the tank and clamber up on to the top to retrieve the unditching beam chains normally stowed in the spud box. With a pocket full of spanners each – in case they drop one – they fix these

chains to the tracks. This done they detach an axe from its location within the spud box and cut the securing ropes that hold the stowed beam in place and, assuming they survive the experience, climb down and re-enter the tank to report that everything is ready.

For the purposes of this description it is assumed that the tank is on an even keel, but that is by no means certain, and if it is slumped over on one side or the other the heavy beam is liable to take on a life of its own once released, so the crew should take this into account. However, for the moment the unditching beam is fastened to the tracks, the crew are safely back inside and the tank is ready to go. The driver locks the differential so that the tracks move in unison, selects the lowest gear and releases the clutch. If everything is working as it should the unditching beam is drawn forwards by the tracks and, passing underneath, fulfils its function and the tank lurches forwards.

Should these slushy conditions prevail on the battlefield it might make more sense to proceed with the unditching beam attached until the tank reaches better ground, although this is likely to put a considerable strain on some components. But if the tank has now freed itself from the trap, and the unditching beam has been restored to its original location, the driver must stop the tank while the beam is detached from the tracks and secured once more to the rails. It is unpleasant, exposed work for those who have to do it and it may well be necessary to repeat the performance if the tank becomes stuck again.

It was a dangerous business. Crew members who had to leave the tank and climb up on top under fire were running considerable risk, so a number of ideas were tried to overcome the problem. In the late summer of 1917 3rd Tank Brigade workshops came up with a system that involved stowing the beam lower down at the back of the tank. The beam still had to be chained to the tracks but at least the crew could work from the ground, with the tank providing some protection. Special wedges welded to the rails also supported the beam and with the beam placed lower down it made the use of a periscope, in the lid of the roof hatch, a lot easier when looking backwards. A securing chain held the beam in place when stowed so, once the special clamps were attached to the tracks, the beam was ready for use once the tank moved off. By reversing, the driver could set the beam back in place so that the crew only had to detach the track clamps and secure the chain restraint as required.

Another experiment, apparently conducted at Bovington, involved two loops of Renold chain running around the tank and driven from an extra cross shaft and sprocket at the back. The unditching beam was permanently fixed to this and pulled around under the tank as necessary. It only needed a clutch on the cross shaft to be engaged to bring the unditching beam around, without anyone dismounting, but one wonders how strong it was in practice.

Finally, there are reports of a full-width cab being fitted at the back of the tank from which crew members could reach the clamps with reduced risk. The feature appeared on the Mark V tank but was said to be tested only in mock-up form on a Mark IV. The cab was evidently fabricated in mild steel at the Oldbury Railway Carriage & Wagon Company works which, given its proximity to Birmingham, suggests the involvement of Major Harry Buddicom, who specialised in work on unditching apparatus and was based in that city.

LEFT The experimental Mark IV fitted with loops of chain to which the unditching beam is attached. The chain is activated by the sprockets on the cross shaft when the external clutch is engaged. The experiment seems to have been initiated at Bovington.

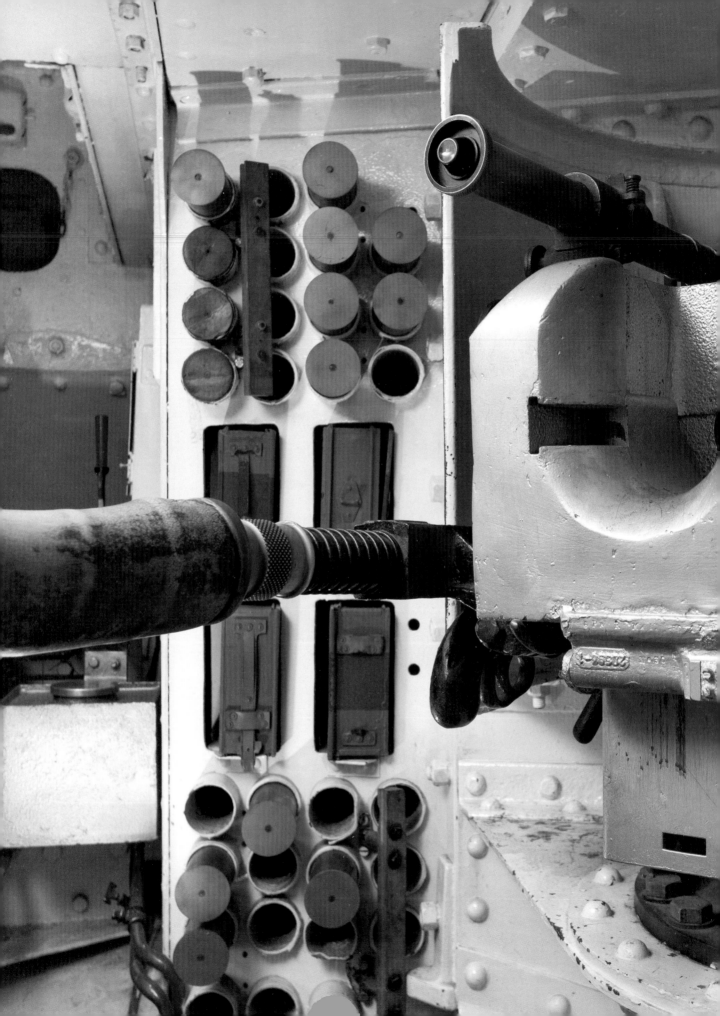

Chapter Three

Tank armament

Today the gun is what the tank is all about, but in the First World War guns were not really the vital factor. It was the very presence of the tank on the battlefield that mattered. However, guns and tanks are inseparable and the strange arrangement from the First World War of having male tanks (mounting 57mm guns) and female tanks (armed only with machine guns) was almost unique.

OPPOSITE **The six-pounder gun station in the Mark IV. The sighting telescope can be seen above the breech, which is in the open position. Ammunition stowage can be seen to the left of the gun and the armrest is extended out.**

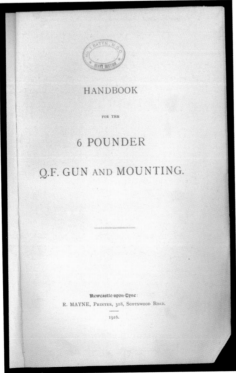

ABOVE A six-pounder tank gun on a training stand, at the Tank Corps Gunnery School at Merlimont on the Channel coast in July 1918. Notice the shield in front, on the ground. It is being inspected by the Prime Minister of Newfoundland who was visiting the Western Front that summer.

RIGHT The title page for the six-pounder handbook of 1916. Notice the rubber stamp of 1st Battalion, Heavy Branch, Machine Gun Corps.

HANDBOOK

FOR THE

6 POUNDER

Q.F. GUN AND MOUNTING.

Newcastle-upon-Tyne:
R. MAYNE, PRINTER, 318, Scotswood Road.
1916.

The main armament of the Mark IV tank, at least the male version, was the ordnance QF 6pdr 6cwt Hotchkiss Mark I or II on mounting casemate special Mark I. The Mark I gun was a single tube rifled weapon with a vertical block sliding-breech mechanism. It was 57mm calibre with a barrel length of 52.12in (1,323.84mm) or 23 calibres (that is to say 57mm x 23 near enough), which has been the traditional way of calculating barrel length in the British artillery. Originally it fired two types of ammunition (or 'natures' to use the military term), high explosive or solid steel shot, which was the closest then available to armour piercing. Later on, a canister shell was added, an anti-personnel round with the effect of a large shotgun cartridge. The Mark II gun was a built-up type but its performance was much the same, as were the other details.

The gun fired a 6lb shot that was permanently attached to a brass cartridge case until it fired, hence the term quick firing,

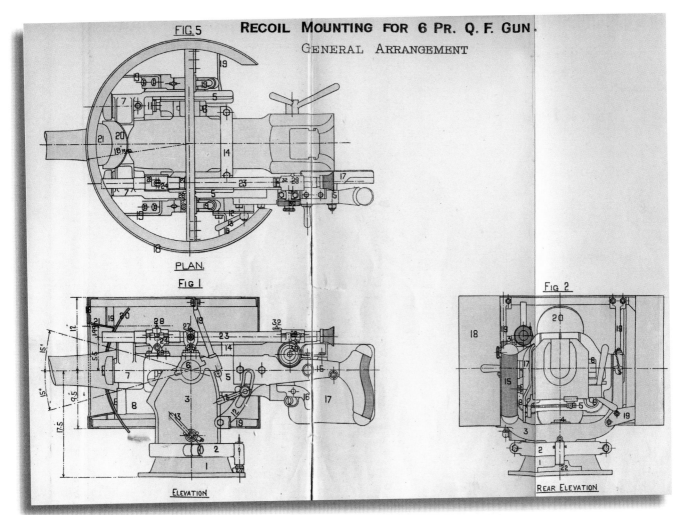

FIG.5   RECOIL MOUNTING FOR 6 PR. Q.F. GUN.
GENERAL ARRANGEMENT

PLAN.
FIG 1

ELEVATION

FIG 2

REAR ELEVATION

ABOVE A diagram from the handbook showing the arrangement of the six-pounder mounting.

and the projectile left the barrel with a muzzle velocity of 1,350ft/sec and a maximum range of 7,300yd, although fighting ranges were invariably a good deal less. It was said to be capable of penetrating 30mm of armour plate at 500yd, which was more than enough under prevailing conditions.

In order to fire the gun the gunlayer stood to the left of the weapon with what is described as the armrest tucked under his right arm. This gave him the leverage necessary to elevate, depress or traverse the gun as required, but

RIGHT The starboard six-pounder in a male Mark IV with the gunner's armrest extended, the butt of the pistol grip underneath and the telescope above.

RIGHT Another view of the six-pounder breech with the armrest folded down.

OPPOSITE Original drawings for shell locker (port side) showing six-pounder ammunition stowage and arrangement of sponson armour.

BELOW A typical six-pounder round compared with a rifle bullet. In fact, this is the highly polished and engraved round, the very first to be fired from a tank.

this armrest could be folded down when not in use in order to reduce the inboard length of the weapon. With his right hand the gunlayer now reached beneath the armrest where he would find a small pistol grip and trigger with which to

fire the gun. The firing action was by percussion and as soon as the recoil cycle was over the loader opened the breech, the empty shell case was ejected and a new round inserted into the gun. The loader, who squatted on the right side of the gun, operated the breech mechanism by a lever on the side, inserted the round, closed the breech and then tapped the gunner on the arm to show that the gun was ready to fire.

The gun was mounted on a pedestal within the sponson, which was bolted to the floor. On earlier and later models a shorter pedestal was fixed to the top of a ready-use ammunition holder within the sponson, but not, for some reason, on the Mark IV. This pedestal was essentially the same as that used on warships, although the recoil arrangements had to be modified to suit conditions inside the tank. The gun recoil was controlled by one hydraulic cylinder on top of the barrel and two spring cylinders underneath.

The mounting and the gun crew were protected by a curved shield that moved with

LEFT Ammunition stowage in a male Mark IV showing the holes for the 57mm rounds and the battens that keep them in place. The oblong slots hold boxes of machine-gun ammunition.

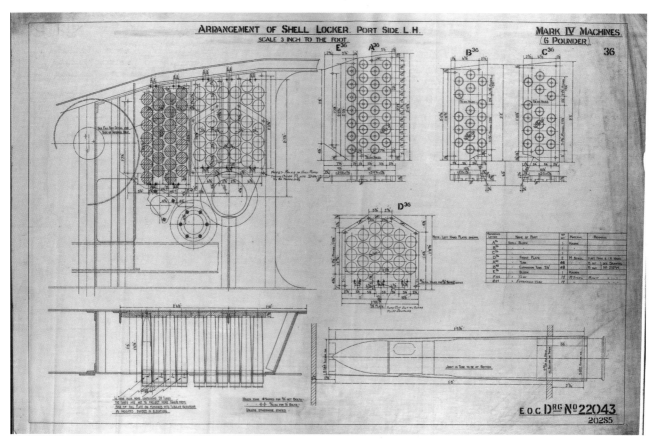

ARRANGEMENT OF SHELL LOCKER. PORT SIDE. L.H.

SCALE 3 INCH TO THE FOOT

MARK IV MACHINES
(6 POUNDER)

36

E.O.C. DRG Nº 22043
20285

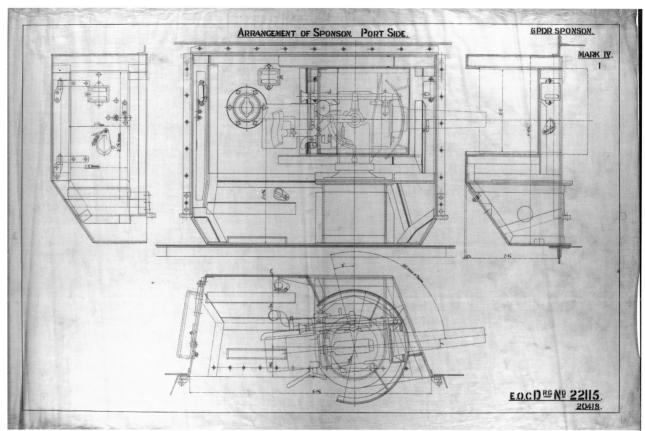

ARRANGEMENT OF SPONSON. PORT SIDE.

6 PDR SPONSON.

MARK IV.
1

E.O.C. DRG Nº 22115
20418.

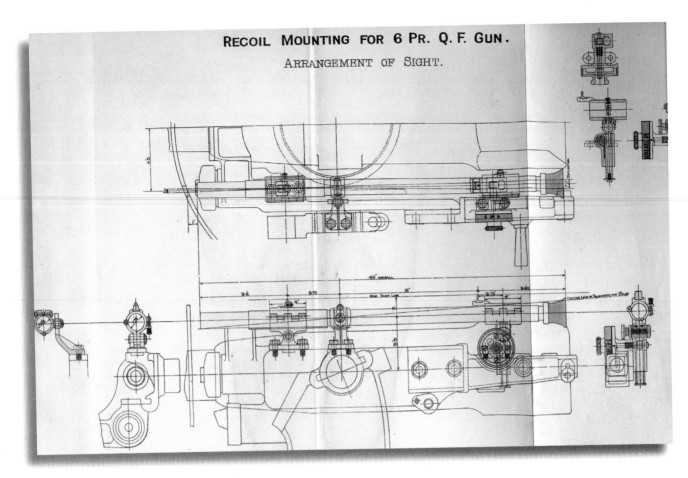

ABOVE The six-pounder handbook also illustrates the bracket that locates the sighting telescope.

RIGHT Webley Mk VI pistol with battle damage. This pistol belonged to Private Walter Carruthers of the Tank Corps. It took the impact of a shell fragment as he carried out a reconnaissance with an officer. Carruthers was convinced the gun saved his life and he survived the war to spend lengthy service in the police.

the gun as it traversed. This shield was 2ft 9in in diameter and 12mm thick, but it had a large slot in it to accommodate the gun and permit elevation or depression, so this in turn was protected by an inner shield attached to the barrel of the gun that moved with it and effectively closed the aperture against incoming fire.

There was a separate, narrower opening in the main shield for the sights, located to the left of the gun aperture. This was not so well protected internally but was slim enough to be missed by anything but a very unlucky shot. A telescopic sight was provided with a x2 magnification. It was fitted to the mounting, on the left of the gun barrel, and moved with it, although the gunlayer was obliged to bend down to squint through it and operate the gun. The sight took the form of a simple brass telescope, 23in long with a field of 20 degrees; it was designed to be pulled apart for cleaning but, due to a difficulty in obtaining proper optical glass, the lenses were made from simpler glass. However, it was described in a contemporary report as 'a very efficient instrument'. Even so,

it should be remembered that experience had shown that long-range firing was exceptional and that fighting ranges were fairly short, so the range drum, fitted to the mounting, was also modified to suit and basic open sights were also provided.

Since the gunlayer could only operate from the left side of the gun, and the loader only serve the weapon from the right, the design of the port and starboard sponsons were not mirror images of one another. The differences are subtle and best recognised by examining the real thing, or relevant photographs. From a practical point of view this meant that even though the arc of fire for each gun was the same – that is, a movement of 100 degrees – only the starboard gun could be trained to fire dead ahead, with an arc that enabled it to sweep around to a point 10 degrees abaft the beam. The port-side gun could not be trained straight ahead but was limited to a point 5 degrees from that position, although it could be turned to a point 15 degrees abaft the beam instead.

The reason for this, aside from the obvious one of squashing a member of the gun's crew,

was to hinder either gun from being fired accidentally and actually striking a part of the tank. To prevent this, special stops were fitted to the turntable, beyond which the gun could not turn, and calculated in such a way as to leave a safe gap of four calibres between the muzzle of the gun and the nearest projecting part of the tank.

Incidentally, in the earlier marks of male tank, Marks I, II and III, which had the longer 40-calibre guns, it was possible for both guns to fire to the front without striking any portion of the tank itself. They were designed in such a way that the lines of fire converged at a point 60yd in front of the tank. A report, issued shortly after the war, explains this by saying that it was not regarded as a problem 'in view of the fact that the Mark IV could be more readily turned than Marks I, II and III'. As all four types used an identical method of steering this is not easy to reconcile, except to the extent that crew efficiency may have improved by this time.

In his book *Log-Book of a Pioneer*, Sir Albert Stern wrote: 'An officer of the Tank Corps, who had once been in charge of the Lewis

FAR LEFT AND LEFT
Port and starboard male sponsons on a Mark IV showing how they differ due to the location of the loader.

ABOVE The .303in Lewis gun. An infantry weapon that became the controversial secondary weapon of the Mark IV male and the primary weapon of the female.

Gun School at St. Omer was responsible for the decision to use the Lewis gun instead of the Hotchkiss. He insisted on it against the advice of the experts in Tanks, who knew the vulnerability of the outer cover of the Lewis gun and the size of its barrel made it very unsuitable for using in a loophole.'

Stern, uncharacteristically charitable, does not name this officer, who was later advanced to the rank of brigadier and given command of 1st Tank Brigade, but it is generally believed to have been Charles D'A. Baker-Carr who had indeed been at St Omer and was known to be an opinionated and forceful man. There was a certain amount of logic in his decision since the Lewis gun was much lighter than the Vickers and did not require such a substantial mounting. But the jacket surrounding the barrel, which was easily damaged and penetrated, proved to be a considerable liability and, what is more, the air flow within the tank, sucking air

from outside to the radiator, reversed the flow of cooling air through the Lewis gun and blew it back into the gunner's face, spoiling his aim and his breathing. Even so, the Lewis gun remained the secondary weapon of the male Mark IV and the primary weapon of the female Mark IV right through to the end of 1917.

In fighting order the Lewis gun weighed 27lb, although in tanks this would have been reduced when the wooden butt stock was detached. The gun fired with a muzzle velocity of 2,460ft/sec and a maximum range of 1,900yd. Its rate of fire was 600 rounds/min, although as a single magazine would only hold 47 rounds, it could not actually deliver 600 rounds a minute with the interruption time for changing magazines. Total Lewis gun ammunition carried in a male tank was 5,640 rounds, or 120 magazines, which were stowed in boxes. For female tanks the total was 12,972 rounds, or 276 magazines, which sounds a lot but might be used up very quickly in intense fighting.

Handwritten annotations to a Tank Corps handbook for the Lewis gun, retained in the Tank Museum archive, mentions armour-piercing machine-gun ammunition being supplied for the Lewis and Hotchkiss guns of Mark IV, Mark V and Medium A tanks. Taken from a General Staff circular and dated 3 June 1918, it is interesting to note that at this time, with the Mark V and Whippet already in service, no attempt had yet been made to adapt the Mark IV to the Hotchkiss gun. However, the circular tells us that in the Mark IV female only, 24 drums or magazines of Lewis gun ammunition would be supplied per tank, suitably painted with the letters AP in white and

BELOW The 47-round ammunition drum for the Lewis seen from above and below with the rounds in place.

Magazine—Top View.

Magazine—Bottom View.

composed, in each case, of alternate armour piercing and standard small-arms rounds in the drum. They were apparently for use against the shields of field guns and anti-tank guns at long range. A certain amount of flexibility was permitted; armour-piercing rounds could be supplied to male tanks if required and, if thought desirable, the arrangement of armour-piercing ammunition per magazine could be altered.

Rather as Stern had forecast, adapting the machine-gun mountings to accommodate the Lewis gun was not a simple task. However, it was solved, and quite brilliantly, by

Frederick Skeens from the Director of Naval Construction's Department. Skeens came up with an armoured ball, held within a two-piece collar with a hole through it big enough to accept the jacket of a Lewis gun. This gave the gunner a tremendous freedom of movement in all directions, but in particular meant that the gun could be aimed and fired horizontally no matter what the attitude of the tank itself. In the early design some kind of shutter was provided to cover the aperture when the weapon was withdrawn, although subsequently a system was introduced whereby the ball itself could be

LEFT A Lewis gun in a Skeens ball mounting in the starboard sponson of a male Mark IV. The length of the weapon and the thickness of the barrel jacket made it very vulnerable to incoming fire. The open sponson door shows the open loophole through which the Lewis gun could be fired in an emergency. The box at the bottom of the door is the means by which empty shell cases were dumped out of the tank.

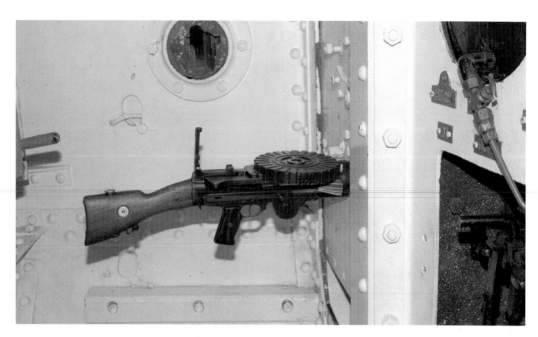

turned to seal off the opening, manipulated by a small handle attached to the ball.

On a male tank there were three of these ball mountings: one in the centre of the cab, between the driver and commander, and the others in the male sponsons on each side and to the rear of the six-pounder position. Female tanks had locations for five guns: one at the front and two each side in the sponsons, where the ball mounting was incorporated within a small rotating shield which, in effect, permitted the machine guns to be aimed along the sides of the tank, front and rear. Another refinement in the male tanks was something like an enlarged pistol port in each sponson door, big enough to accept the jacket of the Lewis gun and with a pivoting cover so that fire could be brought to bear towards the rear of the tank if need be. One imagines that manipulating the bulky gun in such a confined space would not be easy and one questions whether it was ever actually done in practice, but it was possible and indeed was a noted design feature.

The decision to replace the Lewis gun in

LEFT A Lewis gun mounted at the front of the tank, between the driver and commander, the back of whose seat has been removed. Notice how the gun gets in the way of the primary gear lever. It also blasts rather loudly in the driver's left ear when fired.

ABOVE The air-cooled Hotchkiss machine gun as modified for tank use with the tubular stock, ammunition hopper and bag for catching spent cartridges.

LEFT The handbook for the Hotchkiss as published by the Tank Corps centre at Bovington.

tanks seems to have been taken in the summer of 1917, but with active service imminent it could not be done at once and appears to have been postponed until the spring of 1918 by which time new tanks were appearing anyway. The gun selected to replace the Lewis was an improved version of the French-designed Hotchkiss light machine gun, built under licence in Britain and modified to the British .303-inch calibre. However, a lot of contemporary evidence points to the fact that many Mark IV tanks still in service in 1918 retained the Lewis gun as the secondary weapon in male, and the principal weapon in female, tanks.

Hotchkiss machine guns had been adopted as the tertiary weapon in male Mark I tanks,

although at the time the only type available was the Mark I gun, already in use by the British cavalry. It proved less than popular on account of the attached wooden stock, which was regarded as protruding too far into the body of the tank. It also appears to have been a temperamental weapon, firing a 30-round magazine in the form of a strip.

By the following year a new version, the Mark I*, was available, which was readily adaptable for use in tanks. This had a detachable steel butt stock or shoulder piece, giving the weapon an overall length of 47in or 36in if the stock was removed and the gunner held and fired the gun by the pistol grip. The weapon weighed around 27lb and, like the Lewis, had a rate of fire of

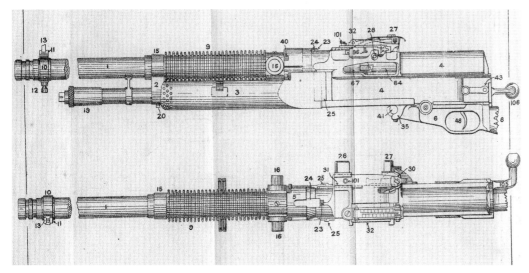

LEFT A diagram from a Hotchkiss manual showing the cooling fins on the barrel and the lever at the back by means of which the gun is cocked.

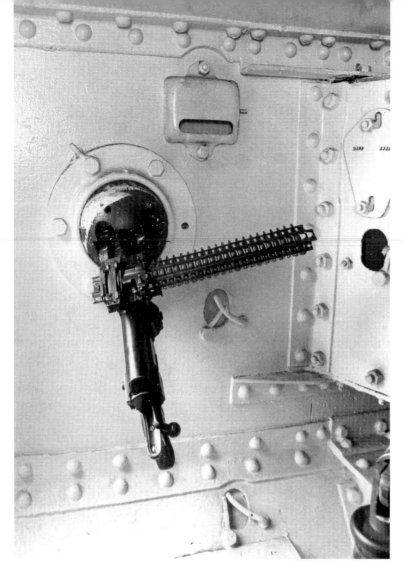

600 rounds per minute. Although it was still possible to use the 30-round strip, feeding from the right, a special hopper was available that contained short, 3-round strips linked together to form a continuous belt of about 48 rounds. Like the Lewis this version of the Hotchkiss also featured a fabric pouch that caught and held empty cartridge cases as the gun fired, even though this was rarely seen in service. The Tank Corps version of the Hotchkiss also came with a small tripod for dismounted use, but there is no evidence that this was often used, if at all.

The Hotchkiss had a maximum effective range of 2,000yd (1,828m) and a muzzle velocity of 2,450ft/sec (747m/sec) and it was manufactured in Britain by the Royal Small Arms Factory at Enfield Lock. Hotchkiss guns supplied for use by the Tank Corps were fitted with a short tubular sight in place of the conventional back-sight, although few visual details of this survive. The Hotchkiss was certainly a lot less bulky than the Lewis gun and remained in service with some British tanks and armoured cars into the inter-war years. In theory, those Mark IV tanks that continued with 7th and 12th Battalions through to the Armistice should have had their Lewis guns replaced by Hotchkiss, with their Skeens ball mountings suitably adapted, but surviving evidence suggests this

ABOVE A Hotchkiss gun, without the stock, in the Skeens ball mount in the port male sponson of a Mark IV, showing the ammunition strip in place.

RIGHT Viewed from the side the reduced inboard length of the Hotchkiss gun stripped of its stock is quite obvious; very important inside a crowded tank.

was never done. The War Diary of 12th Battalion still referred to Lewis guns as late as October 1918, so the chances are that both battalions retained them right through to the end.

The tank man's personal weapon was a six-shot revolver carried in a holster on the belt. Specifically it was the Webley Mark VI, of .455in calibre with a muzzle velocity of 580ft/sec, although the training manual states that it was only accurate up to about 50yd. It offered both double and single action, the latter being preferred for careful, accurate shooting while double action was recommended for close-quarter fighting. The Webley was a heavy weapon, typical of its time, with a fearsome kick and like most British revolvers was reloaded by breaking the pistol, forward of the cylinder, thus exposing the rear face of the cylinder in order to insert new rounds.

There is a persistent whisper, quite impossible to prove, that British tank crews were prone to creating 'dum-dum' bullets by filing a cross in the head of the bullet. Since this was forbidden under international law there are rumours that men were shot out of hand by their captors if found in possession of such rounds. As a result – according to hearsay – Tank Corps personnel tended to throw away their personal weapon, and any ammunition they were carrying, if capture seemed imminent.

ABOVE A restored machine-gun mounting from a female tank showing the elevating and traversing capabilities.

LEFT Aiming a Webley .45 through a protected loophole. In theory this gave the crew the option of firing at enemy soldiers, close to the tank, who could not be reached by other weapons.

Chapter Four

Camouflage, paint and markings

Since tanks were invariably plastered with mud it was not always easy to detect the colour of original paintwork underneath. Tanks were not always painted plain brown; sometimes they were finished in camouflage patterns of more than one shade. Markings ranged from official unit markings to individual names and cartoons, a small selection of which can be seen here.

OPPOSITE The front of the Tank Museum's Mark IV, HMS *Excellent*. The track tensioner is to the right and two of the three-digit number can be seen, three digits indicating a training tank.

ABOVE The Tank
Museum's exhibit,
male tank No 2324,
in the overall brown
finish.

Lodestar III, in the Musée Royale de l'Armee in Brussels, which appears never to have been repainted.

Multi-coloured paint shades, sometimes referred to as harlequin schemes by their critics – intended to break up the outline of an object rather than to blend in with the landscape – were popular during the First World War, and the first tanks were certainly treated in this way. However, by their very shape, and in particular the way the tracks ran right around the body of the vehicle, mud, picked up by these tracks, soon plastered the sides and tended to obliterate the pattern, so this is likely to be the reason why an all-over brown was chosen instead.

Fittings on top of the Mark IV tank are described as being supports for a wooden frame to which camouflage netting was applied. Two brackets on top of the cab, two more about halfway along the roof and two more on the inside faces of the rear horns, intended as a brace for the rear end of this frame, have been identified and may be seen on most surviving tanks, except the Mark V. At the time of writing, no illustration has yet been discovered to show what the frame looked like.

Camouflage netting was commonly used and Frank Mitchell points out that one of its purposes was to break up the shape of the tank, or at least

In his book *Tank Warfare* (Thomas Nelson, 1933), Frank Mitchell writes that 'the highly coloured camouflage painting was abandoned, and all tanks were henceforth of a neutral brown colour'. No date is given, but from other references in that chapter it appears to have been during the winter of 1916–17 when the Mark IV tank was little more than lines on a drawing board. However, with a few exceptions, the Mark IV would also be painted in this 'neutral brown colour', and may be seen most accurately on the Mark IV male tank,

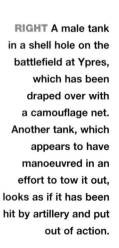

RIGHT A male tank
in a shell hole on the
battlefield at Ypres,
which has been
draped over with
a camouflage net.
Another tank, which
appears to have
manoeuvred in an
effort to tow it out,
looks as if it has been
hit by artillery and put
out of action.

its shadow, when viewed from the air. Douglas Browne, in *The Tank in Action*, describes how, in the days leading up to the Battle of Third Ypres, when tanks were parked up in Oosthoek Wood, camouflage nets were strung from the branches above the tanks and pegged down to the ground, although he writes that in his view the natural foliage was quite thick enough to hide the tanks from inquisitive enemy aircraft. Even so, once the tanks were hidden, crews went to considerable lengths to erase their track marks from the ground leading into the wood.

Browne also makes the observation that camouflage nets and tarpaulin covers for the tanks were so bulky and heavy that they were not normally carried on the tanks when going into action but taken away in lorries. However, there seems to be plenty of evidence to the contrary. For example, Second Lieutenant Alden, commanding G47 at Third Ypres reported that an infantryman shouted to tell him of a fire on top of his tank, which turned out to be his camouflage net, possibly ignited by the exhaust. This was duly extinguished and removed. And even Browne contradicts himself by saying that when he attempted to use a periscope, through the cab roof on the front of his tank, it proved impossible because he had stowed his camouflage net there, rather than in the 'spud' box at the back in case it caught fire from the exhaust pipe.

Other tank commanders, whose tanks broke down or became permanently bogged in a shell hole, normally report that they camouflaged their tank before leaving it. Presumably this was done with a camouflage net, although most do not actually say so and, since a disabled tank was supposed to identify itself to friendly contact patrol aircraft by spreading a white panel on top, this rather negated the effect of the camouflage net, at least from the air.

Whether a tank, draped over with a green and brown camouflage net, could really disguise itself on a battlefield such as Third Ypres – largely flat and, at that time, a sea of mud – is another matter, but a report concerning No 12 Company of D Battalion on 19 September 1917 states that the three fighting sections of the company were sent forward in the dark to lie up in some ruined farms and, on reaching their destinations, 'were camouflaged up as well as possible among the rubble … with brick-coloured camouflage nets which they carried', suggesting some impressive forward planning. The British Army, following the example of the French, had already set up a factory and special works parks in France to advise on such matters and manufacture camouflage nets and other contrivances as early as 1916.

Another common practice, which hardly warrants the name camouflage, involved painting a pattern of black lines on parts of a tank in order to disguise the location of visions slits and other vulnerable points that Germany infantry were instructed to aim at. This seems to have been done very much at the whim of

individual tank commanders or crew, so there is no evidence of a set pattern. And since the majority of tanks carried a variety of official markings in addition to a name, and sometimes a lurid cartoon painted on each side, any sort of camouflage was only viable up to a point.

Visibility from the air was a constant concern, particularly in the Ypres salient in 1917 when German aircraft seemed to dominate. Each tank was supposed to have its number painted on top of the cab to assist British aircraft flying contact patrols, but many crews did not appreciate advertising their presence to the Germans in this way and often smeared the sign with mud in order to hide it. However, many aviators stated that the biggest giveaway from a tank on the ground was the constant flashes from the raised lip of each track link where it caught the sun, although it proved almost impossible to eliminate this.

A photograph of one Mark IV, with a remarkable paint scheme involving multi-coloured stripes and a screen covering the top of the tank and its tracks, is attributed to the artist Ernest Percyval Tudor-Hart, who is also known to have devised camouflage suits for snipers using what appears to be the same pattern. The overhead cover may well have been an attempt to disguise the tracks, but how long it might have lasted on the battlefield is a good question. Another artist who specialised in tank camouflage was Lieutenant

ABOVE C24, *Crusty*, a Mark IV male demonstrates the antithesis of camouflage – its battalion number in white is painted on top of the cab for air recognition.

BELOW The Mark IV female finished in the Tudor-Hart zigzag camouflage and with a net, supported on hoops, covering the tracks. How long that is likely to have lasted is an interesting question.

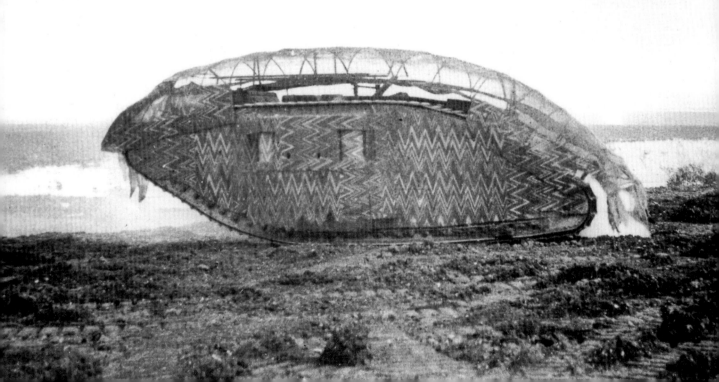

Paget, although he appears to have focused his efforts on creating dummy tanks of wood and canvas.

The antithesis to camouflage is advertisement and this may be found on most British tanks from the summer of 1918 when the Germans began to use captured British tanks. Up to that time the majority of tanks to be seen on the battlefield were British, with perhaps a few French ones, depending on the location. Now with the *beutepanzers* there were enemy tanks on the scene, and the Germans painted large identification markings, such as Maltese crosses, on their own machines in order to advertise this fact. The British response was to daub their tanks, all types, with white/red/white stripes on each side of the nose and on top. Diagrams were distributed to show how

this should be done. However, the degree to which this worked effectively is questionable. The action of 8 October 1918 near Cambrai, where four British Mark IV tanks engaged in combat with four German Mark IV tanks, as described above, suggests that identification markings were not effective at more than 50yd from another tank, but their psychological effect may have had a bearing.

Paint, names, markings and mud – David Willey

The very first tanks were probably painted in a factory coating of 'works grey' or Royal Navy grey, as it was the Navy who funded and led the early experimental developments. In May 1916, the Royal Academician Solomon J.

ABOVE **The Solomon
paint scheme,
recreated on the Tank
Museum's trench
display diorama with
the sole remaining
Mark I tank.**

Solomon, serving as a Lieutenant Colonel in the Royal Engineers, was seconded to the Heavy Section Machine Gun Corps in Norfolk. He was tasked to come up with ideas to help hide the tanks from the enemy, which included a suitable camouflage paint pattern.

Solomon was particularly concerned with shadows cast by the vehicles and creating camouflage appropriate to the landscape where tanks would be used; he proposed 'silhouettes of perforated zinc' to break up the outlines of the tank. He made a trip to France at the behest of Colonel Swinton, the officer charged with overseeing the Heavy Section's development. His quest was to find out more about the local conditions but was frustrated by a lack of cooperation from the Army, who understandably were reluctant to reveal where this secret weapon would first be used. Solomon eventually came up with a paint scheme that was copied by the crews on to

their own vehicles. It consisted of what appears to be four colours, with some of the areas outlined in darker tones. This scheme was later simplified with blocks of colour all surrounded with a thin dark line. Solomon realised 'the camouflage painting of the machine would be effective only in certain conditions, but in dry weather this would be obscured by dust, and in dirty weather by mud'.

The spread of dirt from the tracks running over the machines and the sheer amount of mud created on the Western Front battlefields soon led to the abandonment of camouflage pigment as superfluous. A monotone scheme of brown (often described as chocolate brown) was painted on the tanks from late 1916 onwards. Some Mark II training tanks were fitted with salvaged sponsons from Mark I vehicles and can still be seen sporting the Solomon scheme in early 1917 and at the Battle of Arras in April.

Numbers

Each tank was given a serial number of three, four or later five digits. Numbers were not issued in a logical chronological order but in groups of numbers, not all of which were used. This was evidently to confuse the enemy as to actual numbers of vehicles produced. The Mark IV tanks were given numbers in the following ranges:

2000–2099	Mark IV, male
2300–2399	Mark IV
2500–2799	Mark IV, female
2800–2999	Mark IV
4000–4099	Mark IV
4500–4699	Mark IV
6000–6199	Mark IV
8000–8199	Mark IV

This number was painted on most of the tanks when leaving the factory – usually on the rear flanks of the tank in yellow or white, about 6in high but not all factories carried this out.

Each tank was also given a letter and number for easy reference on the battlefield and for identification, sometimes called the 'tactical number'. This incorporated a prefix letter from the company or battalion the tank served with and the number of the tank in that unit.

Training tanks had a three-digit number. The size, lettering style and position of these tactical markings changed from battalion to battalion and at differing periods in the war. Usually the letter and number were placed on the front side horns, sometimes on the sponsons and occasionally at the rear.

Tanks were also named by their crews, often with the initial letter corresponding to the battalion. For example C Company in 1916 named their vehicles after drinks: *Champagne*, *Cognac*, *Chartreuse*, *Chablis*, *Crème de Menthe* and *Cordon Rouge*.

To aid recognition in battle at Cambrai, tanks designated as wire cutters had WC painted in black on white panels at the rear of the vehicle, for the infantry and cavalry following behind to identify. Supply and baggage tanks had their functions painted on the sponsons, and the few wireless-carrying tanks had WT for ease of recognition.

At least two battalions painted playing-card symbols on the front horns or side sponsons to identify their vehicles. Each company had a colour and within the company each section had a symbol: the first, hearts, the second diamonds, the third clubs and the fourth spades.

One or two tanks sported artwork or cartoons. C47, *Conqueror II*, a Mark IV used at Cambrai, had a caricature of a surrendering German soldier with his hands held aloft.

LEFT The four-digit serial number, unique to each vehicle.

BELOW The tactical number was larger for easy reference. Training tanks were given a three-digit number, issued service vehicles often had a letter (relating to their battalion – A for first, B for second, etc) followed by a one- or two-digit number.

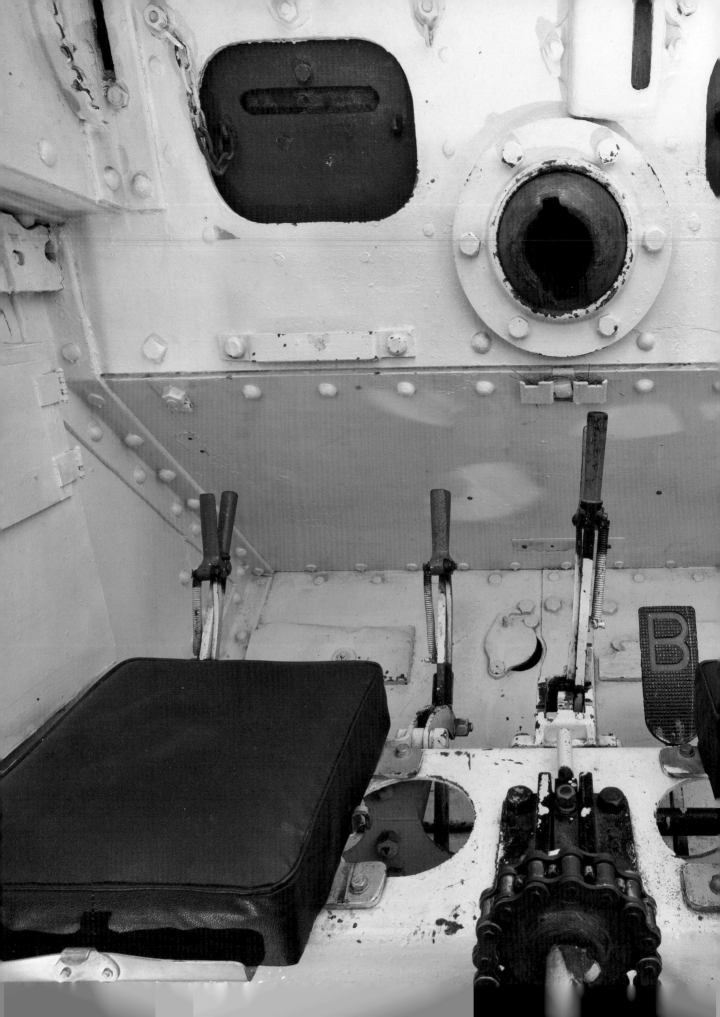

Chapter Five

Operating the Mark IV

◖●◗

It was in the nature of their design that tanks were complicated and difficult things to drive. Out of a crew of eight it required four men to drive a Mark IV tank, and it is important to understand the process because it had a fundamental bearing on how the tank performed in action. Unless this is properly understood the limitations of an early tank cannot be appreciated.

OPPOSITE Facing forward in the Mark IV. The commander sat to the left, the driver to the right.

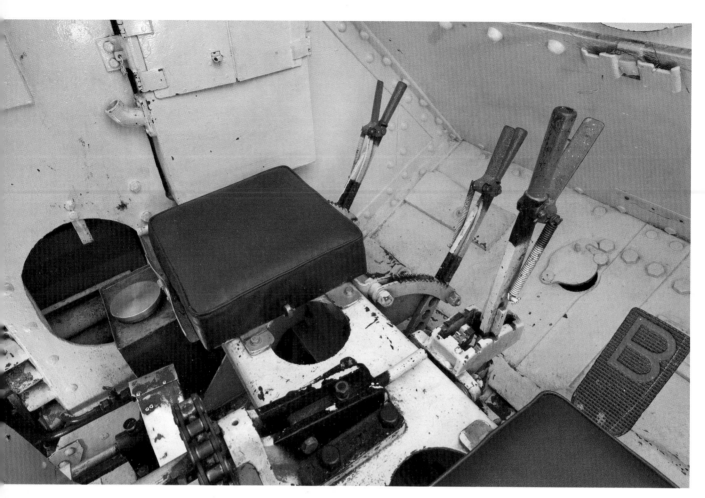

ABOVE Looking across the tank from the driver's seat one can see the primary gear lever and behind it the short, white lever used to engage the starting gear. Also the hole, partially opened in the floor, which enables a revolver to be fired downwards when the tank crosses a trench. The two levers on the far side are the steering brakes.

RIGHT Every vehicle has an operating manual. This is the cover for the driver's handbook.

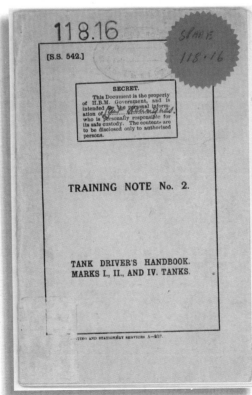

Driving the Mark IV

Writing in 1918 Sir Albert Stern recalled a challenge he made during a visit to Heavy Branch Headquarters in France in April 1917. Based on his premise that tank driving, even in those early days, owed more to the skill and aptitude of the driver than it did to the condition of the tank, he offered a £100 wager to General Hugh Elles, backing a crew of his from 20 Squadron RNAS against any crew that Elles might select to race against them. Elles accepted the challenge but declined the bet, which was probably just as well since the Royal Naval Air Service crew beat Elles's crew by one and a half minutes.

The driver of a Mark IV, or indeed any of those early tanks, was but one of four individuals required to operate it; he could make it go forwards or backwards and select the appropriate gear, but he was unable to steer the tank without help so the success of his driving seemed to depend very much on

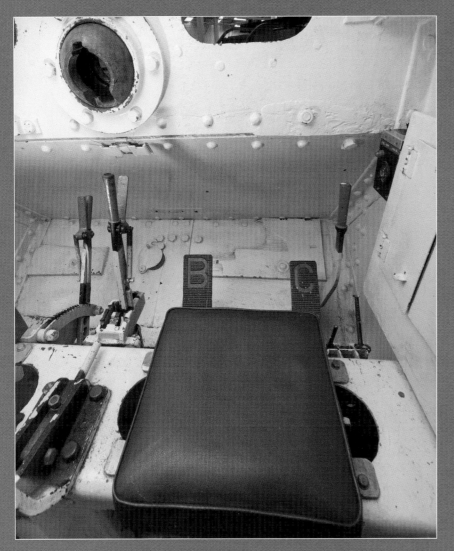

TANK CREW OPERATING PROCEDURE

In order to start the tank the driver (described in the original handbook as the 'leading driver') began by activating a switch behind him 1 on the front end of the engine cover, which brought the magneto and the ignition circuit into play 2. Alongside him, by his right knee were two levers which were respectively the advance and retard lever, 3 linked to the magneto and the throttle lever connected to the carburettor.

When we had to start the Tank Museum's Mark IV (2324 *Excellent*) it was necessary to fill the priming cups atop each cylinder with petrol and then, using the attached tap, drain the fuel down into each cylinder. In the official booklets issued with the Mark IV this process was only recommended as an aid to starting if conditions were poor, particularly if cold, otherwise these cups and taps are described as part of the decompression system.

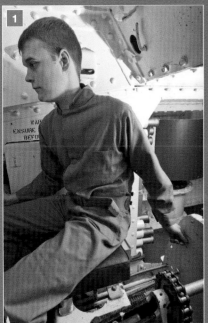

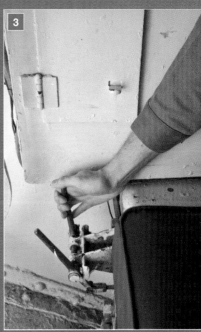

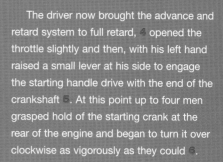

The driver now brought the advance and retard system to full retard, 4 opened the throttle slightly and then, with his left hand raised a small lever at his side to engage the starting handle drive with the end of the crankshaft 5. At this point up to four men grasped hold of the starting crank at the rear of the engine and began to turn it over clockwise as vigorously as they could 6.

This activated a shaft running the full length of the engine that ended in a sprocket and chain drive carrying the motion down to a sprocket in line with the crankshaft, now held in contact by the driver. As soon as the engine fired those on the starting handle let it drop, the leading driver released the engaging lever and carefully advanced the advance and retard lever 7.

It was normal practice to allow the engine to run up for 10min while it warmed up and the oil started to circulate. By the time 10min had elapsed the driver had moved the advance lever to the midway position and the tank was ready to move 8.

The noise inside the tank was now at a dangerous level. It was virtually impossible to hear what anyone else was saying and the crew, hopefully now well trained in their tasks, looked to the leading driver for his signals. The driver had a clutch pedal activated by his right foot and linked to a hand lever held by his right hand in order to provide extra purchase 9. This was depressed and the driver, with his left hand,

engaged first gear in the primary gearbox. Behind him, towards the back of the tank the two secondary gearsmen, probably anticipating his signal, also selected first gear in their respective gearboxes  and as the clutch was released the tank, with just the hint of a jolt, started to move forwards. In fact, given the conditions inside it is not easy for the crew to judge whether the tank is actually moving or not. Only the driver and commander  peering out through the front visors can be entirely sure, because they can watch the tracks moving slowly forwards as they roll around the front idlers.

By now, as the engine itself became hotter, the temperature inside the tank increased and exhaust fumes began to leak from the pipes leading up from the manifold, making conditions inside the tank hardly bearable. In this hot, noisy, fume laden atmosphere the crew could well be working for the rest of the day.

When it became necessary to turn, or 'swing the tank' as the phrase was then, the driver had three options. For a gentle turn left or right he relied on his tank commander, sitting to his left. The commander had his hands on a pair of brake levers that worked on the final drive so that, by hauling back on the left lever for instance , the tank would make a gentle turn to the left, or vice versa if the right lever was pulled. However the

effectiveness of these brakes faded quickly and before long proved to be almost useless, particularly for stopping the tank in an emergency.

To turn quickly, without activating the differential lock, the handbook recommended using the secondary gears in different ratios. For example, in order to turn right the right-hand secondary gear was set in high 13, while on the other side low was selected. Then, with the assistance of the steering brake on the right side, the tank was driven around by the left track, or vice versa if it was necessary to turn left of course. However, experience seemed to show that this method could result in permanent damage to the transmission so that in practice it was discouraged. Of course even this practice, which the handbook described as a method to 'turn quickly' still involved halting the tank in order to change gear, so 'quickly' was only ever a relative term.

The third method, and probably the most common, was to stop the tank, activate the differential lock by a double-handed lever above the driver's left shoulder 14 and then arrange for the secondary gearsmen to select neutral on one side, to which the turn was to be made, and first on the other. Now, with a brake applied to the neutral track and first gear selected in the primary gearbox, the tank would literally pivot in its own length. In order to return to a straight course this entire process had to be repeated, in reverse.

LEFT The commander's seat with the backrest removed. Directly ahead are the two steering brake levers and to the right the primary two-speed and reverse gear lever. Ahead of this is the short horizontal lever the driver uses to engage the crank handle drive, and closer still part of the sprocket and chain that carries that drive down to the engine crankshaft.

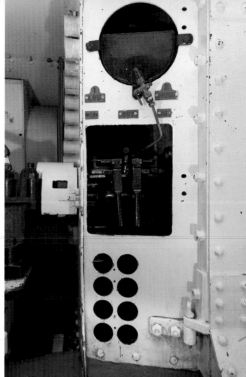

ABOVE The differential casting with the starting crank, painted silver at the front. Also prominent on the right is the linkage that activates the differential lock. At the back one can see the casing for the envelope radiator and the curved shield for the cooling fan. On the left are receptacles for six-pounder shells with the wooden battens that hold them in place.

ABOVE RIGHT The port side secondary-gear controls. Not easy to distinguish inside the dark opening, but the embossed red plates give their function away. Directly above in the round opening is the gravity lubrication tank and the pipe and tap that feeds lubricant to the gears.

the ability of the rest of his team. Yet many of those tank commanders who have written of their experiences pay particular tribute to their drivers and explain the lengths they went to in order to rest these men – during an approach march, for instance – so that they might be ready and fit to undertake the arduous duty of driving the tank in action. Douglas Browne paid tribute to the skill of his 'first driver' in various difficult situations and lamented the fact that sometimes he was obliged to use this man during an approach march, because the going was so difficult. All of which points to the fact that in every crew there was one man who was so much better than the rest at controlling the tank, particularly in demanding conditions. This is probably why, when tanks were withdrawn from the battlefield during the German spring offensive of March and April 1918, their drivers invariably went with them while the rest of the crew, including tank commanders, advanced into the line as Lewis-gun teams.

The secondary gear levers, located in openings in the track frames on each side just to the rear of the sponson openings, were very similar to the gear levers seen on the footplate of a traction engine which, given the peacetime stock-in-trade of William Foster & Co., should hardly be surprising. There were two levers on each side with a toggle device between, which ensured that only one gear at a time could be selected on that side, although since they were

traditional square-cut gears it was never that easy to engage them, even when the tank was halted and the primary clutch depressed.

When neutral was selected on one side or the other during the steering process it was essential to lock the differential and prevent the drive from effectively losing power that way, taking the line of least resistance that under normal circumstances was the natural function of a differential gear. Thus, by locking the differential, drive was maintained to both half-shafts whether in gear or not, so the tank only moved on the driven track. The differential locking lever was fitted to the roof at the rear of the driver's cab, within easy reach of the driver or the commander. A rod from the lever ran back along the roof to a device on the differential casing which, when activated, duly locked the differential mechanism and prevented it from behaving in the normal way.

At the rear of the differential casing, in direct line with the input shaft from the primary gearbox, was a short extension shaft that was set within a brake drum, activated by a shaft attached to the foot pedal in front of the driver. This was the tank's main brake, and very efficient it was too, so long as the drive to both tracks was fully engaged. It was, in reality, a transmission brake but it was only any good – as the crew were reminded in the driver's handbook – if the drive line from the engine to the tracks via the secondary gearboxes was fully engaged. If it

was not then the transmission brake was totally ineffective and, given that the steering brakes operated by the commander were not in perfect condition, as was the normal state of affairs, the tank was liable to run away on an incline with disastrous results. But on level ground there was hardly any need to use the brakes at all. Such was the rolling resistance of the gears, rollers and tracks that the tank was liable to stop of its own accord if the clutch was disengaged.

K (or the 11th Battalion) recorded that by 1918 a Mark IV, in the charge of a skilled driver, could manage to keep pace with a Mark V* heavy tank. Granted the V* was slower than the Mark V due to its extra weight, but it still had the more up-to-date steering system devised by Walter Wilson that enabled a tank to steer more easily and quickly. However, the K Battalion War Diary noted that in competent hands the Mark IV could be turned without having to halt first to change gear. This suggests an experienced crew, rather than just a capable driver, who could go through the gear-changing routine without having to stop, which must have been impressive.

Various horror stories are told of the difficulties of driving at night, on an approach march for instance. Captain Basil Groves of B or 2nd Battalion, who was awarded for his bravery at Third Ypres, and received a bar to his Military Cross as a section commander at Cambrai, related that it was normal practice, at night, for the crew commander to guide

the tank by walking in front of it. This was a dangerous procedure if the commander got caught up in barbed wire, or stuck in deep mud or, worse still, if the driver fell asleep at the controls. Groves reckoned that five or six crew commanders could be killed in this way during an approach march. Groves described a device carried by some officers, which consisted of red and green electric lamps worn on the back and activated by switches accessed on the belt at the front. These could be used to direct the driver, particularly when approaching the start line on the eve of battle when it was necessary to guide the tank around the ends of trenches, parties of men in other defensive positions and other obstacles encountered near the front line.

Presumably not everyone qualified for this rather sophisticated guiding system because Groves also recorded using a handkerchief to dim the light from a lantern or placing one's hand over the glass to produce a dull, red stop light. Major Gerald Huntbach, a Company Commander with H (or 8th) Battalion at Cambrai described using red and green lamps to manoeuvre his tanks into line for the start of the battle next morning. Both officers were very scathing about the effectiveness of the white tape that tanks had to follow. Huntbach said that during his approach march a long section of tape was blown away and he was obliged to act as guide relying on a compass, his memory and a good deal of luck.

The leather helmet used by tank crews comprised of four leather sections riveted together, with a leather chin strap and a lining section with cork wedges to hold it away from the head. These helmets were only used in the first tank attacks and proved unpopular because when the wearer was away from his vehicle he might be mistaken for a German soldier wearing a *pickelhaube*.

This example of a tank crewman's face mask was used by Sergeant S. Dimaschio. When issued, the masks had a small paper label attached that said: 'The curvature of this mask may be adjusted to your face by slightly bending'.

The masks were an attempt to protect crew members' faces from bullet 'splash' – hot fragments of lead or spall from the impact of bullets on the metalwork that found their way into the tank through vision ports or gaps in the metalwork.

Performance

According to official sources, in first gear a Mark IV tank covered the ground at 0.75mph, increasing to 1.3mph in second, 2.1mph in third, with a top speed of 3.7mph in fourth. Not that official figures can always be relied upon. It is clear that some tanks performed a lot better than others due, among other things, to the state of maintenance, the skill of the crew and indeed the effect of gravity on some occasions.

When it came to climbing an incline, as claimed by figures recorded by 4th Battalion Tank Corps, a Mark IV could tackle a gradient of 1 in 2 in dry conditions, 1 in 2.5 in wet conditions and 1 in 4 if it was very saturated. Even so, long, continuous gradients tested the tank, and anything steeper than 1 in 2 was out of the question except for short distances. The design of the track profile, which resulted in what is described today as a high entry point, meant that a Mark IV could deal with a 6ft vertical step or indeed anything up to 12ft high if approached up a slope of 1 in 1. Coming down the tank could cope with a drop of between 12 and 15ft depending on the softness of the ground, although this was tough on the crew if they had nowhere to cling on.

The official figure for trench crossing in the case of the Mark IV was 10ft, although the men in 4th Battalion reckoned that they could deal with up to 11ft. However, a lot would depend upon the nature of the trench; if it had sides which were not firm or regular the tank could become trapped and, as ever, the skill of the driver and his crew would come into the calculation. The 4th battalion also discovered that a Mark IV could wade safely through water around 18in deep although, as Douglas Browne discovered at Third Ypres, once water got into the clutch mechanism the tank was disabled.

Observation and navigation

Fully closed down the tank was dark, hot and noisy inside; so noisy that vocal communication between members of the crew was virtually impossible, although mercifully some external sounds such as the perpetual

impact of machine-gun bullets on the armour plate were also silenced. Yet those bullets peppering the armour meant death or injury to the crew unless they were kept out, so it was essential for some members of the crew to see out – the driver needed to observe the ground in front of him; the commander needed to see ahead too, and be aware of the general situation around him, while the gunners needed to pinpoint their targets.

Various devices were introduced to deal with this. To begin with the driver and commander had large, hinged flaps in front of them that could be opened wide when it was safe to do so, and progressively closed down to a mere slit and ultimately to total closure. At that stage the two men in the cab were forced to rely on very crude indirect vision devices at the front or slim periscopes poking through the roof.

In the early tanks the cab crew were provided with thick blocks of Triplex glass, which was supposed to be bulletproof but under intense battle conditions proved to be anything but. The glass crazed and chipped until it was almost impossible to see through it and there was always the risk of it breaking up and damaging the eyes of the user. It was replaced by a device, rather like a metal pocket, into which fitted two polished strips of

metal that functioned like a simple periscope and were described as reflector boxes. When these strips became damaged the idea was to replace them by sliding out the old and replacing it with the new, but even with good-quality materials the vision provided by this device was very limited.

Both driver and commander were provided

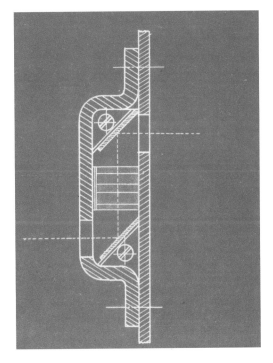

ABOVE Cab of a Mark IV from the front showing the double-flap arrangement of the visors with both flaps partly open. The three slots above and between the visors would have reflector boxes on the inside.

LEFT A sectioned diagram showing a reflector box. The line of sight is shown bouncing off the mirrors. These could be replaced when damaged by sliding them out sideways.

ABOVE Using one of the portable tank periscopes through a revolver port in the rear roof hatch. These could be operated all around the tank, and another position can be seen in the top, right-hand corner of the picture.

LEFT An example of the tank periscope.

with periscopes (usually of a type manufactured by R. & J. Beck Ltd of London); they were in the form of brass tubes about 18in long and were used through holes in the cab roof, held in place by rubber grommets that sealed the opening against rainwater and helped to reduce vibration. They were free to revolve within the

BELOW Drawing of a sector plate showing the six small vision holes that could be brought into line with the slot at the top and the knob that was used to rotate it.

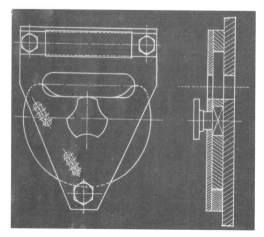

grommet so the commander was able to see in all directions, although his field of vision was restricted. These periscopes were also vulnerable to damage so up to six were issued to each tank so that they could be replaced quickly should the need arise. On most tanks the periscope openings in the cab roof could be covered by bulletproof plates like those attached to revolver ports when not in use.

Although referred to as revolver ports, the protected loopholes that one found all over the tank also served as vision ports, albeit highly vulnerable ones. These ports, of which there were 16 in a male and 17 in a female tank, were roughly teardrop shaped and covered by an armoured flap controlled by a lever on the inside. They were very simple devices and easily worked, but despite being small they were quite large enough to admit machine-gun bullets so it was wise to keep them closed when not in use.

Every crew member was provided with a revolver as his personal weapon and, based upon experience with the early tanks, when enemy infantry attempted to climb on top and try to disable the machine or injure the crew these ports or loopholes could be opened to use revolvers against them. However, there are many accounts of tank crews using the ports to observe the battlefield. The one on the left side of the cab, for example, was popular with tank commanders wanting to detect if other tanks of their section were keeping station with them.

Another vision device found around the sponsons and doors, but not in the cab, might be described as a sector plate, although it was known officially as a revolving peephole cover. In its basic form, as fitted to the Mark IV, it consisted of a metal plate, roughly triangular in shape with a slot near the top, attached to the inner surface of the armour. The slot matched up with a similar one in the armour of the tank itself and between the two was a rotating disc of armour that offered three options to the viewer. In good conditions the disc could be revolved to provide a clear view through all three slots to the outside, but when incoming fire was encountered the disc was turned again so that the slot was filled by a portion of the disc with two groups of tiny perforations, spaced to match the viewer's eyes. The holes themselves were tiny and, contrary to expectations,

provided quite a good view even under fire. The third option, if the disc was rotated again, filled the slot with a blank panel of armour that gave total protection but denied all vision.

Of course, it is one thing to be able to see outside the tank and quite another to know where one was or where one was going. Before setting out, tank and section commanders were briefed on their objectives, on the lie of the land and the nature of the terrain, but certain aids to navigation were provided within the tank. Improbable as it may seem, each tank was provided with a compass to enable it to steer on a bearing, but these appear to have been more trouble than they were worth. Douglas Browne commented on one occasion that his compass had gone berserk. Even when compasses are fitted to large metal objects such as ships they have to be compensated by judiciously placed magnets to counter the magnetic effect of the ship, but in a tank this is aggravated by other factors.

The mass of the tank itself and the magnetism of the engine and ignition system all conspired to upset the compass. Vibration and violent movement did not help and it has even been claimed that simple actions, such as changing gear, could alter the magnetic influences and the accuracy of the instrument. Early tanks from the Mark I up to and including early examples of the Mark IV, were issued with a boat compass, which was gimbal mounted in a wooden box, but it was a difficult thing to find room for and therefore susceptible to damage. It was replaced by an adaption of the Creagh Osborne pattern 259 aero compass, which could be mounted on the interior of the

front cab plate ahead of the driver and within his line of sight. Unlike the boat compass, which had a conventional, horizontal card, the aero compass had a vertical card. Quite why it should be located in front of the driver, who had no direct control over steering, is by no means clear except that the commander probably had enough items to keep him busy.

Each tank was originally issued with a high-quality Watford clock, which was mounted ahead of the commander; unfortunately this seems to have been a much sought after item so it was soon discontinued and tank

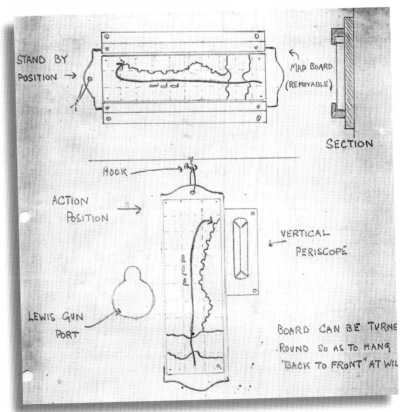

commanders were issued with watches instead. Another item hanging within reach of the commander was a map board, made from wood and used to display a section of map, showing the route that the tank was to follow. The board was suspended by a loop of string so that it could easily be removed and sections of map changed as required. Tank commanders were also taught to recognise surviving landmarks, where such things existed. Douglas Browne, for example, noted a particularly significant tree on the Ypres battlefield and considered the predicament they would be in if it were destroyed.

Other aids to navigation on the battlefield were panoramic illustrations of the skyline – either sketches or photographs – where features such as church spires and other distinctive structures were identified. Douglas Browne regarded these as items of dubious value since they rarely seemed to bear any relation to what could actually be seen and his fellow tank commanders were never able to agree upon what they were looking at.

At a later date surviving Mark IV tanks would be fitted with a Hardings six-figure distance indicator, calibrated in yards and operated from the port driven chain wheel. However, it is not entirely clear where in the tank it was located. One imagines that it would be of more use to the driver or commander than anyone else, but there is no clue on any surviving tanks.

Transport by rail

For a number of reasons such as high levels of wear and tear, and painfully slow speed, tank movement over any distance was undertaken by rail; from the factories to the testing grounds, from the testing grounds to the docks and from the docks in France to the huge Tank Corps workshops and storage facilities in the Ternoise valley, tanks went by rail. Likewise from there to the training grounds or, ultimately to the battle zone, all movement was by train.

To some extent it helped that most of the battles tanks took part in were formal affairs requiring large numbers to be delivered to particular locations. Had the tanks only been needed in small numbers at a variety of locations this would have been much more problematic. Since a tank, complete with sponsons, exceeded the British railway loading gauge, tanks had to be modified to travel this way. Before the advent of the Mark IV this involved unbolting the sponsons and transporting them on special trolleys. But starting with the Mark IV, sponson design was revised so that they could be folded into the tank, thus slimming it down to the point that it conformed with the loading gauge. This could be difficult and dangerous, although as ever crew experience made the task look a lot easier.

To begin with there was a desperate shortage of suitable wagons for transporting tanks. Each tank occupied its own wagon and the normal make-up for a train was up to 12 tank wagons along with other items of rolling stock, including a coach for officers, 2 vans for other ranks, 3 stores vans and 2 brake vans. Most of the available wagons for tanks, whether from British or French resources, were in the 20 to 25-ton class and they did not react well to transporting 28-ton tanks. They had an unfortunate tendency to sag in the middle and after multiple tank-carrying journeys started to fall apart. Suitable wagons were available, notably ones with a 30-ton capacity operated by the Great Western Railway, although these were also in demand for other tasks. Similarly, both the British and French systems operated special wagons for carrying rails that could accept the load, but these too were required for their normal work in addition to being awkward to load due to the long overhang at each end.

ABOVE **After Cambrai, surviving tanks were also evacuated by rail. These may be side-loading wagons.**

BELOW *Auld Reekie*, **a Mark IV male with A Battalion with its fascine prior to Cambrai. It is about to pass across from one wagon to the next, but notice how the wagon it is still on, a French** *Etat* **type, is already showing signs of sagging in the middle under the weight.**

Subsequently, special wagons designed by the Railway Executive Committee and known as RECTANKS, were designed and built in Britain and capable of handling any tank up to 40 tons. The committee also designed a matching four-wheeled wagon that coupled to the end of the train and converted into a ramp, although there is little evidence of any being used at this time. An even more substantial wagon with a carrying capacity of 45 tons emerged in this same period. It bore the codename PARROT but became more commonly known as a WARFLAT. Both RECTANKS and WARFLATS were fitted with built-in screw-down jacks at each end that helped to take the weight when tanks were moving from wagon to wagon along a train.

A number of designs also appeared for portable ramps, although these were probably more useful for offloading a few tanks in out-of-the-way places and were not suited to prevailing conditions in the First World War. Thus the normal practice was to construct semi-permanent ramps from timber railway sleepers and soil; where large numbers of tanks had to be handled, as at Cambrai for example, special railheads with double ramps were created so that tanks could be unloaded side by side.

Getting the tanks on to a train could be a very tricky business except in the rare instances

where a suitable crane was available. The favoured method was to use an end-loading ramp against which the train was parked and over which, one by one, tanks climbed up on to the train, moving along it one wagon at a time until the train was full. At first it was thought that centring the tank on its wagon would present a problem, and highly skilled engineers were approached to devise a means of doing this, but experience showed that a reasonably competent driver, properly lined up to begin with, could achieve this without too much difficulty.

At the destination the train would be shunted against a ramp so that the tanks could be driven off forwards. Bearing in mind that much of this was done at night with minimal lighting it is remarkable that there were not more accidents. Just alongside the road leading from Bovington Camp to Clouds Hill is a concrete platform that represents two railway wagons with a ramp at each end. This was used during the war to train tank drivers in boarding and disembarking from a train.

Although end-loading appears to have been favoured during the First World War there were locations where it was possible to load from the side, although this was never easy with earlier tanks such as the Mark IV owing to the complexity of manoeuvring. It also ran the risk of upsetting the wagon unless carefully done, so under First World War conditions end-loading appears to have been the norm. Experience

showed that a suitable ramp of sleepers with a slope of 1 in 7 could be built by a party of 20 men in 10 hours, and some had to be created quite quickly and then dismantled so as not to interfere with other rail movements more than was unavoidable. It was also found necessary to create a platform of sleepers at the base of the ramp otherwise successive tanks, coming down off a train, tended to excavate a depression in the ground, which became increasingly troublesome as it got deeper.

The build-up for the Battle of Cambrai involved 24 trains, each carrying 12 tanks being moved over a period of 9 days, bringing in the battalions from their various depots to a site known as Plateau, an extensive system of sidings with ramps available to accommodate trains arriving from any direction. At Plateau the tanks were off-loaded, fitted with their fascines, and then driven back on to the trains for onward movement to their forward detraining locations. All of these featured end-loading ramps except two, Bertincourt and New Heudicourt, where tanks had to be unloaded at the side. For this reason trains destined for those locations had to be formed from Great Western Railway wagons code named MACAW B since other wagons, notably the French *Etat* type could not cope with this.

Considering that much of this movement was done at night accidents were relatively few. There were two incidents, on 14 and 16 November involving tank trains. In the first a train struck a lorry on a railway crossing near Ytres while the second involved a wagon full of troops coming off the rails on the approach to Plateau, which caused the death of two men and eight others injured. Contingency plans were in place to cope with any incidents that might occur on the lines from Plateau to the forward railheads. If a wagon was disabled the tank it was carrying had to turn through 90 degrees and climb down off the wagon no matter what damage might be done. It would then be used to drag the offending wagon out of the way so that the broken train could be recoupled and sent on its way. What the lone tank was then supposed to do is not explained.

These rail movements were supervised by the Railway Operating Division of the British Expeditionary Force, but clearly tailored to

the requirements of the Tank Corps and the limitations of the Mark IV tank. Even so, the basic principles adopted at Cambrai served as the model for all future operations where rail movement was concerned. For example, the ramps, although resilient enough to cope with a few tanks, were not robust enough to act as a buffer stop to a 600-ton train, even moving slowly, so a great deal of care had to be exercised at this stage. Tanks also had the ability to damage existing railway lines by driving over them, so careful reconnaissance was essential when tanks had to move around in certain areas.

ABOVE Tanks line up to board a train at the Plateau railhead before the Battle of Cambrai, each one loaded with its fascine. Notice how the ramp has been constructed.

LEFT Railway lines were very vulnerable to damage from tanks, particularly narrow-gauge ones like this. Here a special crossing place has been constructed, but they were not always so lucky.

Chapter Six

The tank at war

Fighting battles was what the tank was all about. Initially regarded with conservative suspicion by the military establishment, in battles like Third Ypres tanks tended to be regarded as an adjunct to the main action. At Cambrai they dominated the battle and pointed the way towards future developments.

OPPOSITE The presence of the tank. This image of the replica Mark IV at the Tank Museum, photographed by Matt Sampson, shows the simple but functional outline of the vehicle to great effect.

RIGHT *War Baby II*, a female Mark IV that served with the Palestine Detachment during the Third Battle of Gaza in November 1917.

Mark IV tank actions

Tanks in the Middle East

BELOW *War Baby II* again, climbing on to a railway wagon in Palestine. There was no real need to retract the sponsons out there because there were no lineside obstacles; however, it made sense to keep the lower doors open on account of the heat.

There is an account that goes back to some of the very first published works on the history of the Tank Corps in the First World War. You will find it in Clough Williams-Ellis's history, published in 1919, in J.F.C. Fuller's *Tanks in the Great War* of 1920 and in a refined form in the semi-official *Short History of the Royal Tank Corps*.

The story, in essence, is that when the first tanks were shipped out to Egypt towards the end of 1916 only old, experimental machines were sent by mistake. Indeed, the *Short History* suggests that Mark IV tanks should have been sent rather than those actually shipped. This last is clearly ridiculous, as no Mark IV tanks were even in existence when the first batch of tanks

left Britain, and the claim that those transported were 'experimental' rather depends on how one interprets that word. What actually happened seems to be somewhat different.

The decision to send tanks out to the Middle East appears to have been based entirely upon the very limited success of the first British tanks on the Somme in France in September 1916. Eight Mark I tanks, hitherto used for training at Elveden in Suffolk and all rather worn and weary, were formed into a detachment of E Battalion under Major Norman Nutt and shipped out to Egypt in January 1917. That Nutt's detachment managed to keep them running at all was not only a tribute to the amount of work that was expended on them but also the discovery that they operated better in sand if no grease was applied to the tracks.

The Egyptian Expeditionary Force, then under the command of Lieutenant General Sir Archibald Murray, was a modest force at that time, working its way slowly east across the Sinai Desert towards Gaza where the Turks had established a strong defensive position. The tanks followed by rail and were detrained at Khan Yunis, too late for Murray's first attack on Gaza but in time for the second, which was launched on 17 April 1917. One tank was lost in this action, followed by two more on the 19th, but in general, despite their age and limited mobility, the tanks were perceived to have been very effective.

In June 1917 General Murray was replaced by General Sir Edmund Allenby whose

LEFT Mark I and Mark IV tanks of the Palestine Detachment, parked up probably after their last battle and awaiting their ultimate fate.

thrusting demeanour, bolstered by considerable reinforcements, gave a new lease of life to the Egyptian Expeditionary Force. The three Mark I tanks written off at Second Gaza were also replaced, this time by Mark IV tanks (two male and one female), bringing the fighting strength of the detachment again up to eight machines. Allenby's only previous experience of tanks had been an unfortunate one, at Arras in April 1917, while his commanders at Gaza had even less. Some seem to have dismissed them as irrelevant while they had strong cavalry forces and plenty of artillery, yet others seem to have swallowed rumour and propaganda wholesale and believed that there was nothing that tanks could not do.

As a result, when the plan was drawn up for their participation in Third Gaza, scheduled to commence overnight on 1 November 1917, each tank was given a long list of tasks and objectives both in the delivery of stores and munitions and in support of the infantry tackling strongpoints in the Turkish positions, all of which they seem to have achieved to a remarkable degree. Although a number of tanks were disabled during the fighting it appears that they were all subsequently recovered and repaired, potentially available for future action.

In the event they were never called upon again. The war in that region resumed its open, more mobile nature better suited to armoured cars and cavalry, resulting in the capture of Jerusalem by the end of the year. According to Basil Liddell Hart (*The Tanks*, Vol 1, Cassell,

1959) the detachment was disbanded and the men, still under Major Nutt, shipped home. The tanks were apparently handed in to an Ordnance Depot but what became of them after that is not recorded.

Third Ypres and the Cockcroft

The landscape around Ypres was largely flat and soon became waterlogged. Tank Corps staff officer J.F.C Fuller railed against fighting there and, in print at least, castigated his superiors for doing so. However, by the summer of 1917 it became almost unavoidable and inevitably, by that time, fighting was bound to involve tanks. As part of the planning much thought was given to cooperation with the infantry, which included a method of signalling to them using a system of coloured

BELOW The Battle of Messines, 7 June 1917, was the action debut of the Mark IV tank and here a group gathers to watch them set off. Note the absence of unditching gear and the even spacing of the track extenders. Huge underground mines, beneath the German positions on the Messines ridge rather stole the tanks' thunder, while the dry going gave a false impression of what was to come.

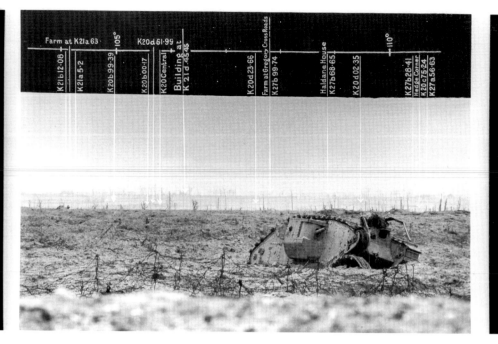

Farm at K21a 63 · 105° K20d 61·99 110°

K21b 12-08 K21a 5-2 K20b 99-39 K20b 00-17 K20 Central Building at K 21 d 45 45 K20d 23-66 Farm at Gregory Cross Roads K27b 99-74 Haldane House K27b 68-65 K20d 02-35 K27b 28-41 Hedge Corner K20 c75-24 K27a 56-63

RIGHT Many tanks came to grief in the salient like this unidentified Mark IV male. It has lain there long enough to become part of a panoramic photograph, annotated with identifiable features. Such tanks would be salvaged or recovered once the ground hardened and it became safe to do so.

discs on sticks. The meaning of the colours was explained in a document issued by the commanding officer of 7th Battalion Tank Corps and included in the Battalion War Diary for July 1917:

■ Green Disc means 'Wire Cut'.
■ Red Disc means 'Wire Not Cut'.
■ Red Disc over Green means 'Have Reached Objective'.
■ White Disc over Red tells the infantry 'Enemy in Dugouts'. [Later on an additional signal

was added: 'Three Red Discs on a stick together indicates "Out of Action"'.]

Much has been written and said about conditions in the Ypres salient and the difficulties of operating tanks there. In places the mud was so thick and so deep tanks were virtually submerged and only made matters worse by struggling to get out. Crews laboured long and hard, digging away mud and scouring the immediate area for materials that could be used to give tracks some purchase or create a ramp for the tank to climb out. This was invariably a futile exercise so the recovery of a ditched tank might have to wait until later when the ground was drier and specialist crews available to effect the recovery. Consequently the Tank Corps gained an unfortunate reputation at Ypres, resulting in a report from 5th Army Headquarters to the effect that tanks were perceived as 'slow, vulnerable and very susceptible to bad "going"'. Since, they concluded, 'The "going" on a battlefield would always be bad' it was suggested 'it would appear that the morale effect of their appearance is diminishing rapidly'. As premature summaries go it was a fine example, but no doubt reflects the general attitude to tanks in the higher echelons at that time.

As a consequence of the mud and the low-lying terrain the construction of effective

BELOW The enduring image of the Ypres salient: water, mud, stranded tanks and forlorn men amid the detritus of battle.

trenches was almost impossible. Instead, the Germans had established machine-gun posts in ruined farm buildings and dotted the landscape with solidly built strongpoints of reinforced concrete. All were christened by the British with suitable names that found their way on to military maps and into common usage among the soldiers.

In this abandoned landscape, the only firm ground was the remains of a pre-war road, if it could be identified beneath the mud. Douglas Browne, commanding Mark IV female tank G46 on 31 July 1917, navigating roughly in the direction of Kitchener's Wood, north-east of Ypres, was well aware of a road a short distance away on his right but had been told that it was probably mined so kept ploughing on through the slushy mud until the inevitable happened and his tank stuck.

Just over two weeks later, on 19 August 1917, Browne was again in action in a female machine, along with eight other Mark IV tanks (two of which were male), against a complex of strongpoints around the devastated village of St Julien. This action, named the Cockcroft after one of the dominant defence works, is regarded as a classic of its kind and relied for its success very much on the fact that for most of the time the tanks kept to the roads, although they were not the secure highways of the present day. Browne describes them thus:

The Poelcapelle road is, or was, a characteristic, straight, continental highway rising very gently uphill from St Julien, lined by fine trees, provided with a deep ditch on both sides and paved in the middle. It had been shelled now very heavily for over a month by one army or the other, or by both at once; and

BELOW Nicknamed *Das Tanktor zu Poelkapelle* by the Germans, 'The Tank gate of Poelkapelle', is shown after the war once the road had been cleared. D32, *Dop Doctor*, is on the left with D24, *Deuce of Diamonds*, tipped over on its side to the right.

ABOVE A location known as Clapham Junction became notorious as a trap for tanks due to the combination of mud and water. This Mark IV male has probably gone as far as it can go.

stood up like a causeway. Of the double line of trees half were down, and a large proportion of these victims lay across the road at all angles. … As we emerged from the village I saw Claughton's tank, fifty yards ahead, surmounting the first fallen tree. A big tree is an unpleasant impediment to a tank, as it is impossible to balance on the rounded trunk and one comes down inevitably on the other side with a jarring crash. On the Poelcapelle road these trees became a dangerous obstacle, because in crashing down over them, with the nose of the tank falling from a great height and the whole thing entirely out of the driver's control, the machine was very likely to slip straight off the greasy pavé which was none too wide, into one of the gulfs on either side. …There also was a danger of breaking a track-plate on the stones. The angle at which the trees could best be taken, lying as they did in all directions, required to be judged, and when this was done they might move suddenly under the tracks and precipitate a crash at the wrong moment.

Not that there is any suggestion that the Germans had deliberately felled the trees to obstruct the tanks – they were down as a consequence of general shelling – but it does go to show some of the difficulties that faced drivers on the battlefield. Of the nine tanks that set out, seven arrived to take part in the

its condition was this. The central strip of pavé had withstood the shellfire moderately well but was badly broken in places by jagged holes. It was covered by a thick, greasy scum and as it was cambered, careful driving was needed if one wished to avoid slipping off. And to avoid this was essential, for the macadamised portions on either side had, for all practical purposes, vanished. They were blown away and merged in the ditches, forming deep gulfs a yard or two wide, out of which the stouter pavé

RIGHT Approaching St Julien during the Cockroft action on 19 August 1917, the tanks had to cross a narrow stream called the Steenbeek. This had been ruined by heavy shelling and one tank, male G4, *Gloucester*, failed to get across.

action which, in tank terms, was not unlike Nelson's tactics at the Nile or Copenhagen. A tank ranged up alongside its objective, as close as it could get without leaving the road, and simply out-gunned it, blazing away with every weapon that could be brought to bear until the defenders gave up. Considering what had been achieved, the cost by First World War standards was miniscule. One tank man killed and fifteen infantry wounded. Browne tells us that for this operation a special system of signalling was adopted; perhaps the coloured discs had not worked. Once a tank had defeated a strongpoint, the signal to call the infantry on to take over was a common or garden shovel, raised aloft though the roof hatch. In this instance, whether they were shy or mistrustful of the tanks the infantry failed to follow up so someone from the tank had to go back and encourage them.

As a result of the Cockroft action the idea of tanks advancing on roads and acting in small groups against limited objectives was regarded very favourably. However, as Browne had forecast, the slippery conditions made it a risky business, based as much on luck as anything else, and this proved to be the case in a number of subsequent actions. Fallen trees continued to be a problem but at least they could be driven over. A disabled tank was another matter. On 20 September 1917 the male Mark IV D44 *Dracula*, commanded by Lieutenant Charles Symonds, broke down on the Poelcapelle road and was abandoned by its crew.

Nearly three weeks later more tanks from the same (D) Battalion moved along the road towards Poelcapelle and were brought to a halt by the immobilised hulk of *Dracula*. Efforts to work their way around it were hampered by the condition of the road and the additional discouragement of enemy shellfire, and in due course five more tanks joined the line of wrecks behind D44. Nevertheless the battle continued but conditions deteriorated under a deluge of continual rain which reduced the ground to a state that precluded the use of tanks, but it was not until early November, when the infantry had struggled up on to the Passchendaele Ridge and taken the village of that name that the British Commander-in-Chief

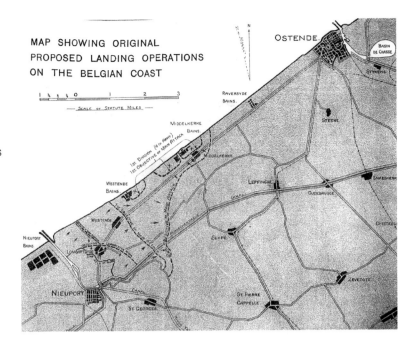

MAP SHOWING ORIGINAL PROPOSED LANDING OPERATIONS ON THE BELGIAN COAST

agreed to call the offensive off. It does not make a particularly edifying story although there were some epic acts of courage and on the fringes the remarkably innovative, if ultimately abortive, amphibious Operation Hush.

Operation Hush, the Great Landing

To a continental army the shoreline represented a secure flank. No other army could work around it without drowning, so upon reaching the Channel coast both sides could relax; the race to the sea was over. There was no danger of being outflanked, so they could concentrate on the problems posed by trench warfare.

To a maritime nation like Britain, however, the sea was a highway and the exposed coastline, behind the enemy line, an open flank. From British shores various attempts had been made to exploit this since 1915 but never with the degree of commitment necessary to make it work. It could not be undertaken except in conjunction with an offensive on land that could link up with it, and the opportunity for that occurred in the summer of 1917 with the opening of the Battle of Third Ypres, which had some ambitious objectives. And 1917, of course, was the first full year of the tank. Not yet a proven and trusted weapon to be sure but one that the British Army was prepared to incorporate into most of its projects on the Western Front, including the innovative Great Landing. This was intended to take advantage

ABOVE A map of a section of the Belgian coast showing the area to be attacked by Special Tank Detachment and 1st Division.

RIGHT Soldiers of the Heavy Section Machine Gun Corps were the first to crew tanks in 1916. They wore the badge of the Machine Gun Corps, shown here. From 16 November 1916 the name was changed to Heavy Branch Machine Gun Corps.

TOP RIGHT On 28 July 1917 the Heavy Branch became the new Tank Corps, with its own cap badge. An earlier design featuring a rhinoceros by Lt Col Swinton had been rejected, but his design for a tank arm badge was adopted for all ranks to wear as a unifying symbol.

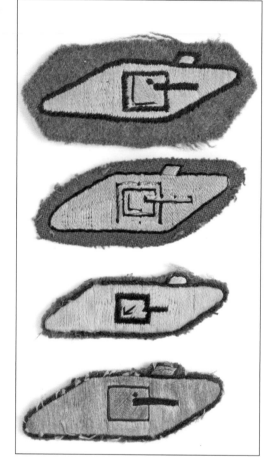

RIGHT Examples of the tank arm badge worn on the right hand uniform sleeve.

RIGHT This faded Tank Corps armlet was worn by Col Henry Karslake. Officers wore armlets like this one when seconded to other headquarters for planning purposes, so they could be easily identified.

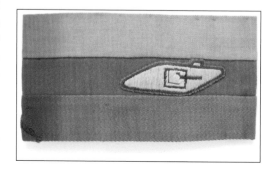

of the Ypres offensive, should it succeed in putting a force ashore on the Channel coast that was strong enough to move inland, seal off Ostend and hold it until the main force arrived. Since it was essentially an amphibious operation it involved General Sir Henry Rawlinson's 4th Army and Admiral Sir Reginald Bacon who commanded the Dover Patrol.

The landing was to be achieved by three enormous pontoons, each 550ft long, which would be pushed through the water and up to the beach by a pair of heavy-gun, shallow-draught monitors that would also provide fire support. The attacking force, drawn from the British 1st Division (Major General Strickland) and including artillery, Royal Engineers and the Machine Gun Corps (with three batteries of the Motor Machine-Gun Corps), was to be divided more or less equally into three, to gather on the pontoons along with three tanks per pontoon; two male and one female, making nine in all. These were formed into a Special Tank Detachment commanded by Major the Honourable J.D.Y. Bingham. All the tanks were Mark IVs and it was a remarkable enterprise bearing in mind that it was still less than one year since tanks had first been employed on the battlefield.

The area chosen for the three pontoons to come ashore was between Westende and Middelkerke on the Belgian coast and, this being a low-lying area, a substantial sea wall had been erected to protect it. Getting the tanks up and over that wall was one of the most challenging aspects of the operation. Sections of a replica wall are said to have been built among the sand dunes at Merlimont, in France, while Lieutenant Colonel J.G.

Brockbank of Central Workshops in France claims that in April 1917 he was instructed to create a replica of a section of the wall adjacent to the workshops.

Three problems had to be overcome. First the tanks had to climb the main body of the wall, which was not likely to be difficult when it was dry but a bit of a challenge if it was coated with slimy seaweed. To cope with this a special track spud of armoured steel was made and attached to every other track link on all nine tanks. The second problem concerned an outward-curving lip at the top of the wall in some places that presented a real problem to the tanks. Various solutions were tried both in Britain and France, the most successful of which took the form of a wedge-shaped ramp on a wheeled undercarriage that was attached to the front of the tank by a bowsprit. This pushed ahead of itself up the slope and was forced beneath the offending lip where it was detached from the tank and held in place while the tank crawled over it. This was the tricky part, demanding skilled driving, but it appears to have worked well enough during trials.

The third problem was quite different. Once the tanks had gained the wall the two male tanks were supposed to move forwards, using

LEFT A Mark IV female fitted with a version of the special climbing spuds, although here used in thick mud rather than seaweed.

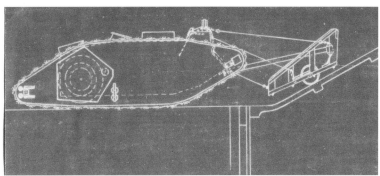

ABOVE The ramp device went through a number of design changes, but this drawing is as clear as any. The location of the winch, which derived its power from the secondary gears, is also shown.

LEFT A poor and evidently doctored photograph showing a male tank propelling its ramp up the sloping face of one of the special training walls.

their guns against the enemy while the female was held back in order to assist other elements of the force to clear the wall. In order to do this effectively these tanks were supplied with power-operated winches, driven from the secondary gearboxes on the right side of the tanks. Design of the winch was reputedly undertaken by John Fowler and Company of Leeds, a firm that specialised in heavy-duty winches for ploughing. The winch drum was mounted vertically on the side of the hull, protected by an irregularly shaped panel of armour plate and wound about with flexible steel wire cable. Thus equipped the tank could haul up tractors, motor vehicles and supply sledges as required. The only identifiable photograph of this arrangement shows tank number 2064 provided with a female sponson on the starboard side. According to surviving records, 2064 was a male tank, built by Metropolitan at Oldbury and it has been suggested that a female sponson was fitted so that the cable from the winch could be led forwards as well as aft. In theory this would not have mattered, since when winching from the top of the wall the tank would be facing away from the sea. However, it is understood that the winch-equipped tanks were later used for tank salvage work when the ability to winch in either direction was an advantage.

This still leaves a number of unanswered questions. For example, all published sources insist that the winching tanks were females whereas, in theory at least, number 2064 was originally built as a male. In the photograph this

tank is shown with the white/red/white stripes typical of a tank still in service in the summer of 1918. In the event it probably does not matter as Operation Hush never took place. Perhaps due to the slow progress of the main battle on land or, as Brockbank for one believed, that it was abandoned because the secret leaked out, the tests having been conducted on a trial ramp alongside a road on the edge of Central Workshops, where anyone could see clearly what was going on. Even so, it was an ambitious scheme and had it succeeded could well have shortened Third Ypres and even given us Ostend. This in turn would have reduced U-boat access to the English Channel with untold consequences for the course of the war.

Tank staff officer Fuller was not a fan; in his memoirs he refers to it as a crack-brained scheme, like a mechanical Gallipoli. In his view the land beyond the beachhead would be intersected by a system of dykes, which the tanks could not cross, leaving the infantry isolated and vulnerable.

Cambrai

The Battle of Cambrai began on Tuesday 20 November 1917 at 06:10hrs.

Further detail of the battle is recounted elsewhere in this chapter, as well as in the sections devoted to 'Transport by rail' (Chapter 5), and 'Flirt II' and 'Deborah' (Chapter 7), but Cambrai is such an important event in the story of the Mark IV tank, and still celebrated today by the Royal Tank Regiment and affiliated

RIGHT A winch-equipped female tank originally designed for Operation Hush and subsequently being used for salvage work.

CENTRE A still from an old film purporting to show Elles with the new Tank Corps flag approaching *Hilda*. His participation in the early stages of the battle is seen as inspirational.

regiments around the world, that it deserves a section to itself.

Indeed, it presents us with an iconic moment in the history of tank warfare and in this battle in particular. Early in the morning, as the tanks were lined up, warming up their engines for the start, a tall figure emerged from the shadows, walked up to tank H1, *Hilda*, and climbed aboard. It was Brigadier General Hugh Elles, commander of the Tank Corps in France, who had elected to inspire his men by accompanying them into battle. As the tank moved off Elles stuck his head out of the hatch on top and unfurled the newly created Tank Corps flag in horizontal bands of brown, red and green; that flag, while not in perfect condition, is still displayed in the Tank Museum at Bovington.

Much has been written about the battle from both sides and it seems to generate just as much controversy, in particular from those advocates of horsed cavalry and the Royal Artillery. It is difficult to make a case for the former as is shown in 'Tanks and cavalry' below. They simply could not survive on a battlefield dominated by machine guns and wire, whereas a tank could, and attempts to usher them through the danger zone to where they might do some good seemed to require more resources than could be justified.

BELOW The only known picture of *Hilda* (a male tank) shows it sheeted down and ready for evacuation at Fins railhead after the Cambrai battle. On the original print the name can be seen on the side, just ahead of the sponson.

The artillery, on the other hand, has a point to make. Since the planners believed that a traditional preliminary bombardment would compromise the element of surprise, the gunners developed a system of accurate and particular target registration based upon the use of map references coupled to mathematically complex surveying techniques. This appears to have worked most effectively and if there was a flaw it may have been in the realms of

communication. Where it might have produced good results, on the ridge at Flesquières for instance where the tanks came under devastating fire from German anti-tank batteries, it was not possible to contact the guns and call back their barrage to help eliminate the risk. Likewise for the individual soldier, faced by a belt of wire and pinned down by enemy machine guns, the distant artillery could not help with his predicament whereas a nearby

RIGHT Another oblique aerial picture taken on 27 July 1917. The Grand Ravin in the foreground was, in practice, little more than a ditch. The spoil heap consists mostly of material excavated for the creation of the Canal du Nord, which is identified on the extreme left and can be seen snaking away to the north.

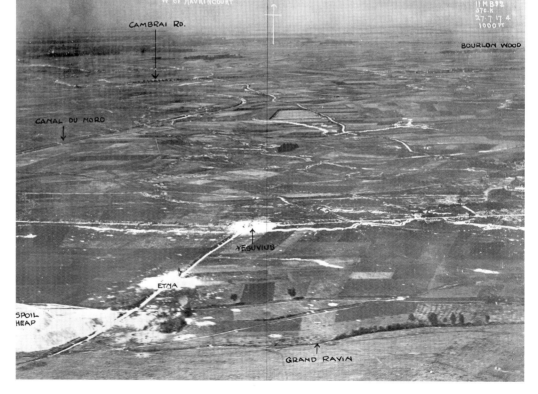

tank could. It shows that there is a place for each weapon in the scheme of things but only if it adheres to its role.

Fuller, who claims to have designed the battle as a raid to demonstrate the potential of the tank – only to have it taken out of his hands at a much higher level and turned into a full scale battle, but one that was planned with a double dose of optimism and very few reserves – says in his book, *Memoirs of an Unconventional Soldier* (Ivor Nicholson & Watson, 1936), that he expected the battle to melt the mental obesity of GHQ, but he was wrong. Fuller was more a military academic than fighting soldier, with a burning belief in the new weapon, while the staff at GHQ were wrestling mentally to fit the tank into a military equation that they could understand. However, at a lower level there was evidence of original thinking. In *Conceal, Create, Confuse* (Spellmount 2009), Martin Davies shows how, in the days running up to Cambrai, six tanks went through a ritual of arriving by rail near Arras. By detraining and moving into a nearby wood from which they surreptitiously departed each night to begin the process all over again, it was hoped that locals would believe that the wood was full of tanks and might pass this intelligence on to the Germans.

The famous case of the locked room in First Brigade HQ at Arras with a notice reading 'No Admittance' on the door gives another insight into tactics employed to deceive the enemy. Inside was a mass of misleading maps and plans strewn about in anticipation that

LEFT Fontaine-Notre-Dame today; the long, straight street, overlooked by buildings on both sides, proved to be a death trap for the infantry and a nightmare for the tanks.

some curious individual would gain entrance and spread inaccurate rumours. The theory presumably was that if enemy attention could be diverted elsewhere there might be no need for reserves. In his book Fuller says that fighting without reserves was like playing cards without capital, pure gambling, and it was the lack of reserves that hindered the long-term outcome of the battle. As it progressed and German resistance increased, the lack of new tanks with fresh crews became a serious problem and there were not enough infantrymen to spare, particularly those with experience of working with tanks, who could sustain the attack. The Battle of Cambrai could be said to have finished on 30 November when the German counter-attack began, but it was effectively over when the tanks tried, and failed, to capture the village of Fontaine-Notre-Dame, which straddles the main road leading to Cambrai. All it did was to repeat on a grand scale what had already occurred at Havrincourt and Flesquières: as the tanks entered the village, the defending infantry

ABOVE B28, *Black Arrow* (commanded by Second Lieutenant J.O. Evans), was one of 13 tanks from 2nd Battalion that penetrated Fontaine-Notre-Dame on Friday 23 November. At least 6 were knocked out by a mobile anti-aircraft gun on a lorry and most of the crews killed. Here a party of Germans pose alongside the tank, which was stopped in the middle of the road, with the body of a British soldier in the foreground.

BELOW Photographed after the battle on 2 December 1917, the long, straggling village shows up well in the oblique aerial view looking roughly north-west. The tracks left by tanks, imprinted on the ground near the little settlement of Anneux, give the best impression of the density of tanks on the ground.

went to ground, only to emerge once the tanks had passed, to open up on the following infantry and drive them back. The scale and intensity of infantry firepower in Fontaine was incredible. One tank is reported to have been sprayed by so much machine-gun fire that every lick of paint was removed, as if it had been shot-blasted; it emerged from the village almost silver. The crew of another tank, a male, reported that fire was so intense that machine-gun bullets came up the barrel when the breech was opened. Fuller, characteristically, has his own take on this. He says that had he known of the danger he would have issued instructions that tanks should bypass villages rather than try to go through them, but this is being wise after the event. Roads lead to destinations and inevitably pass through villages – the obvious way for a tank to go unless instructed otherwise. And was it not the exploit of Stuart Hastie's tank D17 'walking up the Main Street of Flers, with the British Army cheering behind it' that provided the iconic illustration of the very first tank attack in September 1916?

ABOVE Viewed from almost anywhere on the battlefield, the dark shape of Bourlon Wood is painfully obvious. Here it looms, a deep shadow on the horizon, in a photograph taken from the Commonwealth War Graves Commission cemetery in Flesquières.

ABOVE Just outside Bourlon Wood G5, *Glenlivet II*, a female tank commanded by Second Lieutenant Coutts, was blown apart on 23 November.

ABOVE Inside Bourlon Wood two tanks – F6, *Feu d'artifice*, and G21, *Grasshopper* – were knocked out together outside the ruins of the 'Shooting Box', an ornate hunting lodge on the edge of one of the rides through the wood, on the same date.

ABOVE Deep within Bourlon Wood, the same location today but in summer.

BELOW Second Lieutenant March-Phillips's tank, I28, *Incomparable*, slipped sideways and fell into a covered trench on the edge of Bourlon village during the attack on Saturday 24 November. It proved impossible to get the tank out so it had to be evacuated. Here a group of German officers take a cautious look inside.

BELOW On 1 December a number of tanks, mostly from H Battalion, were in action against the German counter-attack near Gauche (or Gaucher) Wood. Here is H23, *Hong Kong*, still lying abandoned on the battlefield after the war. Its commander, Second Lieutenant Viveash, survived the action.

LEFT By the time this picture was taken a new plank road had been created and the Steenbeek become a total swamp. Bundles of fascines had been laid by hand but even that had not been enough to prevent G4, *Gloucester*, bogging down and being abandoned.

THE FASCINE

The fascine is probably one of the oldest military artefacts known to mankind. The word essentially means a bundle of sticks and derives from the Latin *Fascis*, meaning a bundle. The modern equivalent, *Fasces*, was a heraldic device, still to be found on national symbols but was particularly associated with Italian regimes, notably Mussolini's Fascists, who derived their title from the word.

The *Oxford English Dictionary* provides a number of examples of the military use of fascines going back to the 17th century, although by this time the actual bundle could be anything from reeds and twigs to sticks of almost any kind; they were used to fill ditches or swampy areas, build causeways over trenches or other excavations, but were generally of modest size capable of being carried by one man.

They remained a popular item through the First World War and in preparation for the tank attack on the strongpoints north of the Belgian village of St Julien, on 19 August 1917, Captain Douglas Browne records: 'We were

BELOW Without a fascine a tank could drop into a trench at such an angle that it could not get out unaided. This is H45, *Hyacinth*, stuck in a trench near Ribecourt during the Cambrai battle; another tank would be needed to drag it out.

to cross the Steenbeek, not by the ruined bridge at St Julien, but at a point 100 yards to the left, where the engineers that night were going to lay fascines in the bed of the stream.' Today the Steenbeek is a well-mannered stream running between properly maintained banks, but in August 1917 it was the heart and cause of a swamp which spread liberally on either side due to lack of good maintenance, a generous pounding by artillery and rather more rain than the region was used to in summer.

An individual fascine weighed in the region of 45lb but those required for the tanks at Cambrai consisted of 75 normal fascines tightly bound into a large bundle that weighed within the region of 1.75 tons, since they were around 4ft 6in in diameter and some 10ft wide. Large fascines had been suggested as an aid to crossing wider trenches, such as those identified from aerial photographs and more direct intelligence, as existing in the dominant German defence system known to the British as the Hindenburg Line. The Germans had clearly reasoned that if the British tanks had been designed to cope with their standard trenches then wider trenches would defeat them, so the idea was to create a substantial fascine that could be carried by a tank and dropped into the offending trench to provide sufficient support for it and those following to scramble across.

About one month before the Battle of Cambrai Lieutenant Colonel J.G. Brockbank, commanding Tank Corps Central Workshops, was informed by General Elles that a means had to be found to enable conventional tanks to deal with trenches up to 15ft wide. Brockbank claims that the idea of the big fascine and the method of carrying and launching it were all worked out and tested by his people at Central Workshops and that, about two weeks later, he was informed that 400 fascines would be required and inevitably 400 tanks modified to carry and launch them. Attempts to have these fittings manufactured quickly in Britain were defeated by the time available.

Brockbank claims that some 60,000 smaller fascines, each about 10ft long, had to be delivered to Central Workshops and there bundled together to create the large fascines. According to Brockbank, who really should know, between 90 and 100 of these would be required to create one tank fascine, although most other sources claim the quantity was 75. Whatever the truth of this a quantity of the small fascines were placed in a cradle, wrapped around with chain and then compressed using two tanks, pulling on the chain in opposite directions until the dense bundle of fascines was creaking under the pressure. The loops of chain were then secured with shackles, detached from the tanks and rolled over a sea of mud by a group of 15 to 20 Chinese workers from 51 Chinese Labour Company, who then loaded them on to railway wagons for onward despatch to the railhead.

Meanwhile, the work of adapting the tanks to carry and launch the fascines was also a Central Workshops responsibility. Internally this involved fitting a lever at the back of the cab, within reach of the driver, which activated a quick-release mechanism, and a pair of hooks on the front edge of the cab. These hooks engaged with a wooden railway sleeper, embedded in the base of fascine to hold it in place. Two lengths of chain ran around the fascine to the external hook of the quick-release lever behind the cab but attached to the nose of the tank at the front where two other hooks were located.

Tanks and fascines met at the plateau railhead; one by one the tanks dismounted from their trains and were matched up with their fascines. Although a crane was provided to lift each fascine in place, the normal practice was to raise the fascine via chains joined to the tracks, with the tank reversing until the fascine was in place. For the next stage the fascine was rolled back and secured on top of the cab and only shifted forwards to the launching position, perched on the lip of the cab, when going into action.

A special drill for using the fascines within the complex of the Hindenburg position was

ABOVE *The Tank*. A watercolour by Frank Brangwyn (1867–1956). The watercolour shows *Hyacinth* from H Battalion ditched in front of Ribecourt on 20 November 1917. Compare this painting with the photograph on the opposite page taken at the time. Although never an official War Artist, Brangwyn created over 80 posters during the First World War and painted a huge oil on canvas called 'A Tank in Action' as part of a rejected scheme for the Royal Gallery at the Palace of Westminster. It is now part of the National Museum of Wales Collection.

worked out by the then Major J.F.C. Fuller involving groups of three tanks. Fuller tells us that there were not enough tanks in France to create the ideal arrangement of four tanks per section. While the leading tank, still with its fascine in place, ran along the first trench, firing down into it, the two other tanks each used their fascines to move deeper into the trench system. Should everything go as

BELOW I51 on a tank train at Plateau railhead with its fascine in place on top of the cab. One can just see the end of a sleeper poking out at the base.

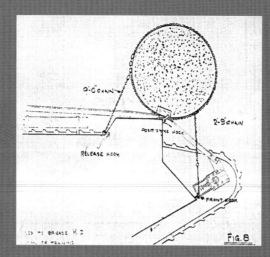

RIGHT An official sketch showing the carrying and release arrangements for the fascine, although in reality it was not as neat as that.

planned the first tank would now follow the others over the fascines they had dropped and plant its fascine in the third-line trench. Unless a tank had been disabled or suffered mechanical problems all three tanks should now be through the first trench system and be ready to join up with the second wave, moving across, unless reserves of fuel or ammunition were seriously depleted.

Using a fascine for trench crossing is described well by a tank commander of E (5th) Battalion commanding a male Mark IV tank in the first wave: 'The Hindenburg Line was a truly formidable obstacle and we naturally had a few exciting moments. First, poised over the deep and wide excavation; then, releasing the fascine – would it drop alright? – we saw it lumber beautifully to the bottom. Could we get over? One can imagine our doubts as we had witnessed a few ghastly failures at Wailly. …'

Some accounts include a member of the crew dismounting to plant a flag on the edge of the trench, indicating the precise position of an available fascine for following tanks; one mentions a red and yellow flag being thrown out of the tank for the same purpose.

It is as well to affirm at this point that the fascine was a one-off device as far as each tank was concerned. Once dropped it could not be replaced nor recovered. Not just because of the physical difficulty of lifting it back out of the trench but also because it was needed for use by other tanks. Not only that, but by the time it had been driven over by a succession of tanks it was in no fit state to be used another time. In fact there is no evidence to show that fascines were ever used again. Apart from there being no requirement in the immediate future, no tank action on the scale of Cambrai took place again before Amiens on 8 August 1918. By then things had changed.

For the 1918 battle Central Workshops devised a new device, christened the crib, which worked on the same principle as the fascine and was carried by Mark IV and the dominant Mark V tanks used at Amiens. However, it was not required for the longer Mark V star tanks, nor was it applicable to the smaller Whippet tanks, which had not really been designed for trench crossing in the first place.

The crib was a manufactured item, created from timber and angle iron bolted together. It was approximately the same size as a fascine but a good deal lighter. There is no evidence that the weight of a fascine seriously inhibited the movement of a tank, although its location – at the front – must have affected the centre of gravity to some extent, but it was unlikely to be used for any length of time.

The crib, being lighter, was unlikely to affect any tank that carried it and, in theory, there was the added advantage that it could be dismantled after the battle and used on subsequent occasions as required. But Captain Browne, who saw service as a reconnaissance officer at Amiens, had a very poor opinion of cribs, remarking that they tended to buckle and collapse when a tank crashed down on one and clearly believed that the old 1917 fascine was far superior.

BELOW A Mark IV female carrying a crib, the 1918 replacement for the fascine. This tank broke a track during the crossing of the Canal du Nord in September 1918.

Tanks and cavalry

Major Clough Williams-Ellis described the German wire entanglements at Cambrai: 'In front of the main (trench) line lay band upon band and acre upon acre of dense wire; nowhere was it less than 50 yards deep and here and there it jutted out in great salients flanked by batteries of machine-guns. Never had we before been faced with such a wilderness of wire.'

It had already been discovered that a British heavy tank of the time, driven into the wire, could crush it down sufficiently for a foot soldier, stepping high, to cross it in the wake of the tank. But it was also noted that should another tank attempt the same thing a few yards away the wire formerly pressed down sprang up again.

Although infantry could cope by being fairly adaptable it still presented a serious obstacle to cavalry: a single strand of barbed wire was enough to injure a horse. There are those who defend the use of horsed cavalry in the First World War and usually point to their effectiveness in the Middle East against the Turks as justification. But on the Western Front it was another matter. In addition to barbed wire one had to consider small-arms fire – in particular the massed use of machine guns – shelled ground and trenches, all of which inhibited cavalry in their principal role, which relied on mobility and shock action. Indeed, the Oxfordshire Hussars, the first yeomanry regiment to be deployed on the Continent, were starting to question the value of horses and mounted operations on a modern battlefield as early as 1914, even before permanent trench lines and barbed wire had become established.

However, the British cavalry had served the nation well. They were replete with history and glamour, and many senior commanders, from the Commander-in-Chief Douglas Haig downwards, were all born and bred cavalrymen with a vested interest in the *arme blanche*, which appeared to dominate and sometimes skew their thinking.

To be fair there was a case for the cavalry working in conjunction with tanks at Cambrai. The belief was that if the tanks and artillery could smash their way through the German defensive system the mounted arm could then

gallop forth into the open country beyond, in the traditional manner. As a result three divisions of cavalry were earmarked for the battle with the idea of sweeping around Cambrai, faster than any tank could go, containing the garrison and advancing north-east to the River Sensée, preventing German reinforcements from interfering.

The trouble was, of course, to get the cavalry across the battlefield and into a position where they could engage the enemy, as Sir Douglas Haig said in his despatch of 20 February 1918: 'With no wire and prepared defences to hamper them, it was reasonable to hope that masses of cavalry would find it possible to pass through, whose task would be thoroughly to disorganise the enemy's system of command and inter-communication.'

Reasonable maybe, but practical? The battle simply did not turn out like that and in the event the cavalry's contribution to the success of the battle was minimal. Only a few horsemen managed to cross the St Quentin Canal, and none ever set eyes on the River Sensée or anywhere else east of Cambrai, except as prisoners of war; certainly not in 1917 anyway.

It is a measure of the importance still accorded to the cavalry that of some 476 tanks available for the Cambrai battle no less than 32 were earmarked for the role of wire-pullers to pave the way for the soldiers on horseback to reach the action, where Haig expected them to do their damnedest.

A wire-pulling tank was a conventional Mark IV fitted with the Top Towing apparatus as

ABOVE F1, a 6th Battalion female tank, crashing its way through the wire and crushing it down during training at Wailly.

RIGHT A grapnel, recovered from the Cambrai battlefield, showing the heavy-duty shackle that attached it to the cable and the tank.

BELOW A tank almost engulfed in wire during trials. The grapnel can be seen near the top, on the right.

BOTTOM Wire such as this presented no obstacle to a tank, but it could stop cavalry. This is F1 at Wailly again.

described in the 'Supply tanks' section above. Those that have been identified so far all appear to be females. Each tank was provided with a four-pronged grapnel, often referred to as an anchor, which it dragged through the wire at the end of a 10m-long cable. Swivels between the end of the cable and the grapnel itself permitted the latter to twist as it went, winding the uprooted wire into a strong, tangled skein.

The wire-clearing tanks were organised into three groups, which were to advance and begin their work after the second line of fighting tanks had moved off. Their task was to clear a 60yd-wide gap in each belt of wire they came to and, in the gaps between the belts of wire, the grapnels were to be carried on the petrol tank at the rear of each tank. However, lifting it from the ground was a challenge due to the weight and in a report prepared by the officer commanding the wire-pulling detachment he doubted whether it could even be done at all under fire.

On approaching a belt of wire the dedicated tanks arranged themselves in pairs, side by side, cast off their grapnels, straightened out the towing hawsers and plunged into the wire. Advancing steadily ahead, they began to tear the wire away. Dragged along at the end of its hawser the grapnel slowly turned in its rotating shackle, twisting the wire into its strong mass. Examination of the ground afterwards showed that every last vestige of wire, along with the wooden or iron stakes that supported it, had been swept up.

As the report shows, the system worked best in the thickest wire, which in general appears to have been the German wire. Nobody ever found out quite how much wire could be removed in this way since the tanks were limited to lifting 60yd at a time although the implication is that a tank could drag off a lot more wire if it had to. Once this amount had been pulled a releasing device was activated and the tank detached from the grapnel, which was now deeply tangled in wire. At this point a pioneer soldier appointed to the task and attached to each tank, cut the wire away from the grapnel, releasing it for further use.

While steering, or 'swinging' was to be avoided if possible when towing the grapnel, trench crossing was strictly forbidden – practice had shown that the release gear that let go of the grapnel was too weak and sensitive for the task and could be activated by any bump or violent movement. Such was the importance attached to their role, the wire-pulling tanks were not expected to take part in any offensive actions. However, as they were armed and the instructions included the requirement that one gunner should be stationed on each side of the tank at all times, they were, nonetheless, ready to engage any suitable target that came within their view.

Once their special tasks were completed and two of the three routes for the cavalry were cleared up to selected points on the St Quentin Canal, the vehicles were not required to continue as fighting tanks and went no further. However, pairs of tanks from each section working on the other, northern, route – which would take the cavalry on to the River Sensée – carried extra fuel and water, and were to accompany the horse soldiers to do further wire clearing as required.

In fact the cavalry were never able to take advantage of all this work – apart from one adventurous foray across the St Quentin Canal achieved by B Squadron Fort Garry Horse in 5th Cavalry Division – and most of the horsemen found the intense activity on the battlefield too much to handle and tended to maintain a low profile. The British Official History accuses the mounted troops of a 'lack of enterprise' at this point. A contemporary view of the cavalry, albeit by a tank man, is summed up in the oft-quoted passage by Major Philip Hammond of F Battalion. Hamond had just witnessed the event when one of his tanks F22, *Flying Fox II*, commanded by Second Lieutenant W.F. Farrar, attempted to cross the damaged girder bridge at Masnières only to prove so heavy that the structure subsided beneath the tank, dropping it gently into the stagnant canal amid a cloud of steam.'Then', said Hamond, 'a most ludicrous thing happened. There was a great deal of clattering, galloping and shouting and a lot of our medieval horse soldiers came charging down the street. I yelled to them that the bridge was gone but they took no notice of me and went right up to it. They turned about and came trotting back with a very piano air.'

Two tanks attached to the wire pullers were

used to carry and deliver bridging materials for the cavalry to a dump near Gouzeaucourt, while other troops, mostly dismounted Indian cavalry serving as pioneers, cleared, levelled and filled in ditches and trenches to complete the cavalry tracks.

While the cavalry have their defenders one feels that, like Haig himself, their views are coloured to a large extent by sentiment. Few things appear to indicate the futility of cavalry operations in modern warfare more than the idea of valuable tanks and infantry being sidetracked to prepare sanitised routes across the battlefield for soldiers from another age.

The time of the Savage Rabbits

The role of the British tank in the First World War was to assault the enemy defences. It used its weight to crush down barbed-wire entanglements, its size and shape to clamber over the trenches and its armour plate to resist machine-gun bullets while carrying the weapons to fire back once among the enemy. It was also painfully slow, partly because it was underpowered but also as its main purpose was to break down the German trench system and lead the attacking infantry through.

ABOVE The new bridge over the St Quentin Canal at Masnières, which replaced the one destroyed by *Flying Fox* on 20 November 1917. It was near here that Philip Hammond had his encounter with the cavalry.

LEFT Wire was no serious obstacle to a tank. It could either squash it down or drive right through it. Odd strands might get caught up in the grousers, but they invariably snapped and if the worst came to the worst it could always be cut away.

RIGHT Tanks
abandoned on the
roadside at Brie-sur-
Somme, caught on the
wrong side of the river
by the German attack,
with a Mark IV male in
the foreground.

By January 1918 the Allies had come to the conclusion that the Germans were building up their strength for one last, massive breakthrough attempt in the west, which would divide the Allies and bring the war to an end in their favour. The collapse of the Russian regime and war machine released huge numbers of men for the Western Front and the Germans were believed to be building tanks of their own design and refurbishing numbers of British tanks, captured at Cambrai, for their own use.

All this was understood at Allied Headquarters, but what they could not do was forecast when, or indeed where, the blow might fall. Work went ahead creating strong defensive positions, preparing bridges for demolition and

planning how to combat the German assault. But what could be done with the tanks, what part might they play? Clearly they could not be held back in reserve and launched once the German line of attack could be identified; they would never get there in time. And although three Tank Corps battalions were in the process of converting to the new and faster Whippet tanks, the majority – at least ten battalions in France – were still equipped with the Mark IV tanks, which had neither the speed nor the flexibility to fend off an infantry attack. It was probably the last time that most battalions of the Tank Corps would be equipped with the Mark IV.

On 21 March 1918 – preceded by one of the most mind-numbing artillery bombardments of the First World War, unleashed along a 40-mile front – waves of enemy storm troopers swept into action. The effect was stunning and a number of 'backs to the wall' messages were issued to the Allied troops, although in fact as far as the Germans were concerned it was a lost cause. Even the toughest men can only go so far on their feet, and if supplies like food, water and ammunition fail to get through they can fight no further. At the same time the Allies were falling back on their resources and, although they took staggering casualties, they also shortened their defensive lines and brought this final German push to a grinding halt.

BELOW More
abandoned tanks of
5th Battalion unable to
return across the river
from Brie-sur-Somme.

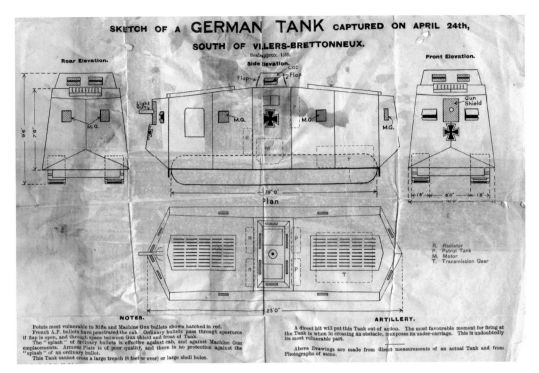

SKETCH OF A **GERMAN TANK** CAPTURED ON APRIL 24th,
SOUTH OF VILLERS-BRETTONNEUX.

Scale approx. 1/50.

Rear Elevation.   Side Elevation.   Front Elevation.

NOTES.
Points most vulnerable to Rifle and Machine Gun bullets shown hatched in red.
French A.P. bullets have penetrated the cab. Ordinary bullets pass through apertures if flap is open, and through space between Gun shield and front of Tank.
The "splash" of ordinary bullets is effective against cab, and against Machine Gun emplacements. Armour Plate is of poor quality, and there is no protection against the "splash" of an ordinary bullet.
This Tank cannot cross a large trench (8 feet or over) or large shell holes.

ARTILLERY.
A direct hit will put this Tank out of action. The most favourable moment for firing at the Tank is when in crossing an obstacle, it exposes its under-carriage. This is undoubtedly its most vulnerable part.
Above Drawings are made from direct measurements of an actual Tank and from Photographs of same.

R. Radiator
P. Petrol Tank
M. Motor
T. Transmission Gear

LEFT A chart compiled following examination of one of the abandoned A7V tanks at Villers-Bretonneux. A bit distorted but enough to show British tank men the salient features.

It was agreed that if the tanks could not go to the enemy then the enemy should come to them, so the idea was conceived of planting small groups of well-camouflaged tanks in forward areas, close to where the attacking Germans were expected to come, ready to attack them when the opportunity arose. General Elles called this 'like Savage Rabbits [emerging] from their holes' and the practice became known as the tactic of the Savage Rabbit. On occasions it worked quite well but it was a costly business. Many tanks had to be destroyed when bridges were blown that cut off their retreat, and Major Clough Williams-Ellis, in his history of the Tank Corps published by *Country Life* magazine in 1919 reckoned only 180 out of 370 tanks that were fit to fight actually saw action. His view, as an experienced officer serving with 1st Tank Brigade, was that it would have been much better 'to give the Tanks a run for their money'.

The Germans, though, did just that, so far as it was possible. On the morning of 21 March 1918 five A7V *Sturmpanzerkampfwagen* of 1st Assault Tank Detachment along with five captured Mark IV female tanks of 11th Assault Tank Detachment were deployed against British lines west and south-west of St Quentin. The attack began in thick mist, made worse by the volume of smoke from the artillery barrage, and was of limited duration. Of the five German machines only two survived to the very end of the action but they were instrumental in driving British troops out of a number of positions and capturing many more. The five seized British machines, although generally proving more reliable, were too slow to keep pace with the infantry. Once visibility improved the German storm troopers struck out and the tanks simply could not keep up with them. Indeed, it seems that they were also too slow and unwieldy to avoid fire from British artillery and two were damaged.

The action got poor coverage in British accounts and was frankly doubted by some writers, notably Clough Williams-Ellis. Since the majority of British soldiers who encountered the

BELOW An artist's interpretation of the action between Mitchell's Mark IV male and Leutnant Biltz's A7V, *Nixe*, near Villers-Bretonneux on 24 April 1918.

gun. They were grouped in detachments of 12 guns, although the nature of the fighting meant that a number of these crews fought, and died, in isolation. Many at the time regarded this as wasteful employment of skilled men, but these were desperate times.

The Canal du Nord

Far from the narrow, contour-hugging old English canals with their crude hand-worked locks that date from the Industrial Revolution, the waterways of France and Flanders are generally broad and deep and are still a significant part of a modern communications system. They would pose an effective obstacle to tanks even today.

In 1917 the Canal du Nord was still under construction – although work on it had been suspended due to the war – and it represented a major obstacle on the battlefield at the time. The stretch that snaked between Ruyaulcourt in the south up to Inchy formed, in practical terms, the western boundary of the fighting zone during the Battle of Cambrai. By 1918 the Germans had reoccupied much of this ground and done their best to render the dry canal an even more effective tank obstacle. So much so that the British plan called for some old tanks, of no further combat value, to be prepared to form a causeway, from bank to bank, that the fighting tanks could use to get across.

ABOVE A Tank Corps Lewis gun team normally consisted of three men, although when in the line attempting to resist the German onslaught they would not be as isolated as this picture implies.

tanks were either killed or captured no verifiable reports were received at the various British headquarters; however, it seems that in general the reaction of British troops, confronted by enemy tanks, was no different to that displayed by the Germans – this was a new and terrifying aspect of warfare for the men of all sides.

From about 24 March, when countless tanks had already been lost, dismounted crews, of whom many survived, were organised as Lewis-gun teams to serve with the infantry. Each team consisted of three or four men and one Lewis

RIGHT Another view of a Lewis gun team trying to make themselves comfortable in the line. Again the group consists of an officer and two men.

The attack that was launched on 27 September 1918 actually began a week earlier when the tanks began moving forward; 7th Battalion, Tank Corps, one of just two battalions still equipped with Mark IV tanks, set off from their base to the village of Morchies on the night of the 20th, having to cover 11,500yd to get there. It was followed by five days of rest and refit before setting off again on the 26th to cover another 6,000yd to a place called Pronville, from where they would go into action the next morning. The tanks had moved the best part of 10 miles on their own tracks – something that would hardly have been considered possible a year earlier. Yet the tanks were the same, and indeed it was thought that some of these rejuvenated veterans had fought in the first Cambrai battle of November 1917.

But the biggest challenge of all still faced them – the formidable Canal du Nord. Given the distance of the approach march it is perhaps no wonder that the older tanks that were to fill the canal all broke down on the way, so if the fighting tanks were to get across they would have to do so under their own power.

Since it was such a daunting obstacle Tank Corps intelligence officers consulted original civil engineers' drawings of the canal while the Royal Air Force flew risky photo-reconnaissance missions to provide the best possible information for the attackers. Three specific crossing points were selected, none of them easy but the worse by far was that due east of Inchy-en-Artois, near the present Lock 4. The official Tank Corps publication, *Weekly Tank Notes*, reported that it was successfully crossed by five Female Tanks, all carrying cribs. The earth banks were extremely steep – much steeper than indicated on the drawings. Probably they would have been considerably flattened out in finishing as they could not be considered as permanently stable at such a pitch. The Tanks concerned negotiated the further bank with surprisingly little trouble, probably due to the earth covering of the brickwork.

All the above Tanks were Mark IV, and a few of them had fought in last year's (1917) CAMBRAI battle. All the obstacles were taken at right angles and not obliquely.

ABOVE Tanks gathered in the bed of the Canal du Nord show what a formidable obstacle it was.

LEFT The Canal du Nord near Lock 4 looking south as it is today. The water gives a false impression of the depth of the earthwork.

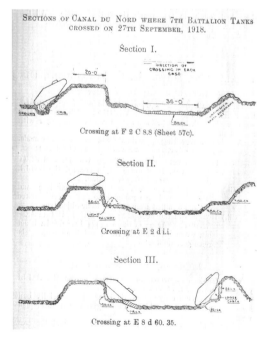

SECTIONS OF CANAL DU NORD WHERE 7TH BATTALION TANKS CROSSED ON 27TH SEPTEMBER, 1918.

Section I.

Crossing at F 2 C 8.8 (Sheet 57c).

Section II.

Crossing at E 2 d i.i.

Section III.

Crossing at E 8 d 60. 35.

LEFT Profiles showing sections of the Canal du Nord where tanks crossed. The location was by Lock 4 near Inchy-en-Artois.

The nature of this operation is further emphasised in the following citation, taken from the *Tank Corps Book of Honour.*

201299 Pte. POTTINGER, MAURICE WILLIAM. 7th Battn. Awarded MM.
For conspicuous gallantry and devotion to duty.

On the morning of September 27, 1918 he drove his tank across the Canal du Nord, south-east of Inchy. At this point the banks were extremely steep and considered by some an insuperable obstacle to a Mark IV tank. He reached the wire with the infantry and led them to Quarry Wood. As the tank was not supplied with prisms or periscopes, he drove throughout with his flap open although under very heavy machine-gun fire.

When clearing up trenches on the Red Line the tank, while under a barrage, developed mechanical trouble. Pte. Pottinger showed great resource and skill in rectifying this. He has driven skilfully throughout the whole of five actions since August 21st.

Clearly Private Pottinger mastered the steep side of the canal and then proceeded to do good work during the attack on Quarry Wood, en route for Bourlon village. Since four other Mark IV tanks crossed the canal at the same place it obviously took more than this

to qualify for a Military Medal. While fighting in Bourlon village, on the edge of Bourlon Wood, some tanks are reported to have created a smokescreen. This may be connected with a statement in the 7th Battalion War Diary for September 1918 that on some tanks at least 'smoke gadgets were fitted to the exhaust', which may refer to a system developed in Britain whereby a thick cloud of smoke could be emitted if sulphonic acid was injected into the exhaust.

Since there is no account of a return crossing of the canal it must be assumed that the surviving tanks rallied on the west bank, from where B Company set out on the following day to support the Canadians in their attack on Bourlon Wood and a subsequent advance to the Marcoing line, which they all reached. Two days later, on 30 September 1918 six Mark IV tanks supported 7th Canadian Brigade in fighting around Cambrai that resulted in two tanks being disabled and another being surrounded and captured by the Germans. It may not have been realised at the time, but this was the final action of 7th Battalion, on ground over which they had fought successfully just 11 months earlier. The battalion history explains the situation concisely in a paragraph from the *Narrative History of 'G' and 7th Tank Battalion* that might stand as an epitaph for the Mark IV.

RIGHT A stretcher party following a Mark IV female tank through a gap cut through the embankment on the eastern side of the Canal du Nord.

THE DÉBACLE

The enemy's retirement from Cambrai after these actions proceeded so rapidly that Mark IV tanks were unable to keep pace with it. The Battalion was pushed forward in two echelons, one going as far as Ramillies, and the other following behind it to Tilloy; but the tanks did not get in touch with the retreating armies. On October 12th the Battalion was withdrawn into G.H.Q. Reserve. The tanks assembled near Fontaine Notre Dame, and on the 27th were entrained at Havrincourt for Erin, where next day they were returned to Central Workshops, the Battalion going to Blingel Camp.

Even so, this was not quite the end of the story. The 12th Battalion of the Tank Corps, the only other element of the Corps still to be equipped with Mark IV tanks, was also on the Cambrai battlefield, further south, while the 7th conducted their epic crossing of the Canal du Nord but were not in action. The general opinion at Brigade Headquarters was that the Mark IV would not be capable of dealing with the wide trenches of the Hindenburg Line, yet although the Tank Corps was now equipped not only with a new generation of tanks but inevitably a new generation of men who had not experienced Cambrai in 1917, the unpublished war history of the 12th Battalion states that 'Mark IV tanks had crossed it successfully the previous year, and there really was no reason why they should not cross it again'.

Beutepanzers

On 24 April 1918 a section of three tanks, one male and two female belonging to No 1 Section, A (1st) Battalion Tank Corps, were ordered forward from the Bois d'Aquenne to confront an approaching wave of Germans who had already driven Allied troops from the town of Villers-Bretonneux and were threatening the city of Amiens. The section was command by Captain J.C. Brown and the male tank by Second Lieutenant Francis Mitchell who due to the effect of gas could only muster a crew of five men instead of the usual seven. Their instructions were to advance towards a section of trench known as the Cachy Switch Line and hold it at all costs.

Mitchell tells us that at their destination he was unable to locate any infantry, until a man

ABOVE A soldier artist's impression of the first tank versus tank battle at Villers-Bretonneux on 24 April 1918. Frank Mitchell's tank is said to have been A1, so whether A3 is artist's licence or a mistake cannot be verified. The German A7V has been rendered with a good deal of latitude and the tanks are shown much closer together than accounts imply.

sprang up from a trench, waving his rifle and shouting 'Look out, Jerry Tanks about.' Captain Brown, who was travelling in Mitchell's tank dismounted and went to warn the two female machines while Mitchell manoeuvred to locate the German machines. There were three of them, moving steadily forward, and closest was

BELOW German tanks were rarely seen, even this close, although this photograph was said to have been taken during a training exercise.

Sturmpanzerwagen 561, *Nixe*, commanded by Leutnant Biltz of Abteilung II.

Inevitably when relying on reports from two opposing sides one has to accept that there will be differences. Mitchell claims that having spotted *Nixe* two other German tanks could be seen further away to the left and right. German authors say that there is no evidence for any other A7V tanks to be there, in company with *Nixe*; had there been, the outcome of the battle might have been very different.

It would appear that Mitchell saw the German tank first. To Biltz in *Nixe* the brown British tank was difficult to distinguish against the looming background of the wood from which it had emerged, and Biltz claims that he first became aware of the presence of British tanks when he caught sight of the two females making off towards Cachy. Mitchell saw them too: ' I noticed to my astonishment that the two females were slowly limping away to the rear. Almost immediately on their arrival they had both been hit by shells which tore great holes in their sides, leaving them defenceless against machine-gun bullets and as their Lewis guns were useless against the heavy armour-plate of the enemy could do nothing but withdraw. Now the battle was to us.'

Since Biltz is unlikely to have hit them, with the damage inflicted by his 57mm gun not sufficient to do such harm as Mitchell describes, presumably the shells he mentions were fired by artillery. Mitchell also states that his tank was peppered by machine-gun fire, which he assumes came from *Nixe* but the odds are in favour of it having been an infantry weapon.

Mitchell's gunner was suffering from the effects of gas and working without a loader and the tank was pitching like a ship in a rough sea making aiming difficult but, having swung the tank around so that the left gun would bear, and noting that rounds were striking the ground in front of the German tank, Mitchell risked halting his tank to give his gunner a better chance to aim. He counted three hits although the citation for the Military Cross he won in this encounter gives the number as five:

Second Lieutenant Mitchell, Francis. 1st Battalion. Awarded MC.

For most conspicuous gallantry and devotion to duty in action against enemy tanks at Cachy on April 24, 1918.

This officer was in command of a male tank in action east of the Cachy Switch Line, when the hostile tanks came into action. He fought his tank with great gallantry and manoeuvred it with much skill in order to bring the most effective fire on the enemy one, but to avoid offering a greater target than possible.

As a result of his skilful handling of his tank and his control of fire he was able to register five direct hits on the enemy tank and put it out of action.

Throughout he showed the greatest coolness and initiative.

In the end the result of this action would probably qualify as a pyrrhic victory. Biltz evacuated his tank at once, fearing that it might catch fire and explode, while Mitchell remained patrolling in his Mark IV until it was hit by a German mortar round and disabled, whereupon he and his crew dismounted and made for the nearest trench. Meanwhile, since *Nixe* had not exploded Biltz led his crew back aboard and nursed the tank back behind the German lines. According to Biltz once he was aware of the proximity of Mitchell's

BELOW The first step in recovering a disabled British tank involved jacking it up, placing special rollers underneath and then towing it away. This photograph, taken in Bourlon village shortly after the battle, shows a German recovery team using a big compound traction engine to move a Mark IV female tank.

BOTTOM At the improvised railhead the tank is jacked up again, the rollers moved away and a railway wagon shunted underneath.

RIGHT H48, *Hypatia*, though, was found abandoned, then recovered and returned to service, but this time in the German Army. The six-pounder gun is about as far as it can go and may be damaged, but it would be replaced with a German gun in any case.

tank he had ordered his gunner to fire at it, yet Mitchell does not record any hits apart from some armour-piercing machine-gun bullets that wounded a member of his crew but probably did not come from *Nixe* anyway.

Since the Germans never built more than 20 of their own *Sturmpanzerwagen*, the main strength of the German tank force rested on seized and rebuilt Mark IV tanks recovered from the field of Cambrai (*beutepanzers*, meaning 'captured tanks') and it is their story that engages us now, continuing on from the saga of *Flirt II* after it was captured in Bourlon village on 27 November 1917. *Flirt II* was one of 50 tanks recovered by the Germans of which 30 were deemed worth putting back into operational condition – 12 male and 18 female. The remainder were to be dismantled as a source of spare parts or used as 'hard targets' in order to investigate the resistance of their armour.

The Germans had identified a site near Charleroi, in occupied Belgium, which became the headquarters of the *Bayerischer Armee-Kraftwagen-Park 20* (BAKP 20) responsible for the recovery and restoration of tanks. A large factory, Ateliers Germain, to the west of the city at Monceau-sur-Sambre was used to store and refit the tanks while a location somewhat north-east of Cambrai, called Lieu-Saint-Amand, was adapted to resemble a Western Front battlefield for driver training.

It is ironic that F13, *Falcon II*, which had been trapped in Bourlon village by *Flirt II*, should

BELOW A view inside the Ateliers Germain factory *at* Monceau-sur-Sambre, Belgium, where captured British Mark IV tanks were put back into working order or stripped for spare parts.

LEFT The Germans set up a tank training area at Lieu-Saint-Amand in France, where crews were taught to handle British tanks over a variety of obstacles; this male Mark IV is tackling a steep bank, watched by young officers.

the original identity of most of the tanks they rebuilt – although such information would probably only be of interest to historians. Even so, it seems unlikely that *Flirt II* would have been returned to fighting trim on account of the damage it had suffered.

Of course all this is impossible to prove and indeed there is no trace of *Flirt II* from the time the tank is damaged and abandoned in Bourlon village in November 1917 until its appearance at the front of the Tank Museum after the Second World War, always assuming that it is the same tank. Where had it been all that time?

It seems safe to assume that following its recovery *Flirt II* was taken to Monceau-sur-Sambre but after that it is lost to sight. Given its condition one imagines that it was only ever used as a source for spare parts, although there is evidence that another tank H48, *Hypatia*, had its battle damage repaired and saw active service. What is more its identity was confirmed because the Germans failed entirely to obliterate its name with their paint scheme. Could this have happened to *Flirt II*? It is not impossible but it does appear to be a lot of trouble to go to under the circumstances.

The evidence seems to show that in total the German tank force managed to field about 30 *beutepanzer* IVs, split between six battalions, albeit probably not all available at the same time. The majority were female tanks,

ABOVE F13, *Falcon II*, was used by the Germans to make a film and then shown to the Kaiser at Le Cateau. The unditching beam does not seem to have been secured.

become a bit of a star, at least for a while. It was shown to the Kaiser (Wilhelm II) at Le Cateau in December and to members of the staff of Army Group Rupprecht at the same time. It also appeared in a German film about the 'English' tanks at Cambrai in which it is seen trying to push over a tree. Yet in the end it was F4, *Flirt II*, that survived, or appears to have done.

Thorough as they were in most respects, it seems that the Germans failed to record

RIGHT A recaptured male tank fitted with the German Maxim-Nordenfelt 57mm gun, which looks very similar to its British counterpart.

FAR RIGHT This Mark IV female, probably photographed during training at Lieu-Saint-Amand, carries a water-cooled Maxim machine gun in the forward mounting, although this does not appear to be common.

RIGHT Tanks were then finished in a colourful camouflage scheme and sent by rail to the training ground or direct to Assault Tank Detachments at the front.

like *Falcon II*, but the German plan to rearm them with water-cooled '08 Pattern Maxim machine-guns failed so they were equipped with captured Lewis guns reworked to accept German 7.92mm ammunition. Male tanks were to be equipped with 57mm Maxim-Nordenfelt cannon that were so similar to the British six-pounder that it hardly made any difference. However, this modification, which also involved a new pedestal for the gun and added protection around the sponson opening, took such a long time to implement that very few captured male tanks ever saw action. This may be accounted for by the fact that fewer male tanks were seized anyway – perhaps because of their tendency to catch fire and explode when hit, due to the nature of their ammunition, although numerically, male tanks were never as numerous as the female version to begin with.

German sources claim that the British tanks were much more cramped than their own A7V model, but it should be borne in mind that in German service a Mark IV tank carried a crew of 12 or 13, compared with just 8 men in British service. At some stage a compass was installed into the cab roof of each captured tank, the same type used in the Germans' own tank, the A7V *Sturmpanzerwagen*. In practice it seems to have been unreliable, needing continual adjustment due to the mass of metal nearby, but it was also considered vulnerable to the unditching beam when it was used; so on many of the captured Mark IV tanks the rails supporting the beam were raised a few centimetres above the roof of the cab to clear it. All things considered, the Germans were singularly unimpressed by the British Mark IV tank; the fact that it worked and did what was expected of it seems to have escaped them. However, if there was one thing that British and German engineers could agree on it was the inadequacy of the steering system. The fact that two extra men were required to work the secondary steering gears was hardly ideal and the Germans reputedly attempted to solve this

problem, although it is not surprising that their efforts did not work.

On leaving the Ateliers Germain factory the tanks were painted in a colourful, somewhat gaudy camouflage scheme of clay yellow, green and a reddish-brown in patches but, in case this was not enough, they were liberally covered with black crosses and in due course unit identification marks and names. Because the tanks were so slow and not attuned to the pace of their infantry the Germans relegated them to a follow-up role, dealing with targets that the infantry had bypassed and the artillery had missed. However, it has to be said that when faced with attacking tanks British infantry were just as likely to leave the area as quickly as possible as their German counterparts had done a year earlier.

The Germans organised the *beutepanzers* into Assault Tank Detachments, numbered consecutively after those already earmarked for their own heavy tank, the A7V. Assault Tank Detachments equipped with captured British tanks consisted of five vehicles, two male and three female, although the supply of reworked male tanks depended upon the availability of suitable 57mm guns.

But as far as the Germans were concerned the war situation was deteriorating daily and

BELOW Female tank L52, *Lyric*, of 12th Battalion was probably captured later since it retained most of its British markings. After the war the French emplaced it as a tourist attraction near Le Fort de la Pompelle. The fittings on top, the two tie rods and the hefty block indicate that at one time it was adapted for hauling sledges. It would be known to the Tank Corps as a 'Top Towing' vehicle, the idea being to keep the towing cable away from the tracks.

by the middle of October 1918 orders came to evacuate the facility at Monceau-sur-Sambre and move back to Germany. New premises at the MSN factory at Gustavsburg, near Mainz, had been selected.

In fact they had left it too late; events were moving more quickly than could be imagined and when the Armistice came into effect on 11 November 1918 everything was still at Monceau-sur-Sambre and British troops were not far away, at Mons. In the event it was not until 28 November that the first British troops were seen in the area, six Austin armoured cars of 17th (Armoured Car) Battalion of the Tank Corps under Captain May, although they were more concerned with local security than investigating an abandoned factory full of wrecked tanks.

The situation at Monceau-sur-Sambre is unclear. Serviceable tanks would presumably still be with the troops, leaving only those in need of repair, or those retained for spare parts on site. Whether *Flirt II* was one of these is not known, but unless this tank had been restored and put into service it must have been one of the cannibalised hulks which one assumes had not been repainted, thereby making it possible to see its original identification. However, under the circumstances, this was not a time for keeping precise or accurate records so some speculation is necessary.

After the signing of the Armistice in November 1918 three captured Mark IV female tanks were retained and used by elements of the Freikorps in their struggle against the nascent communists or Spartacists in what amounted to a civil war. Tanks were seen on the streets of Berlin from January 1919, attached to a unit commanded by an officer with wartime tank experience. By May they had been transferred to Leipzig and attached to a unit known as Kokampf, but they were rarely used and when the Germans agreed to sign the Treaty of Versailles towards the end of the following month they were obliged to dispose of all surviving tanks.

Even so, one Mark IV female tank had been shipped to Stuttgart where staff at the Daimler factory were using it as an example from which to create a German version of the Mark IV. It was kept hidden, only venturing out in an emergency, and was not surrendered until 1920.

As far as is known nothing came of the Daimler project, not to be confused with the rhomboid-shaped A7V-U, which developed a nest of troubles. Based upon other experience it seems that whatever Daimler developed after examining a Mark IV would be over-engineered to the extent that it was likely to be unworkable. It would not have the crude simplicity of the British design.

RIGHT After the Armistice the Germans retained a few tanks and issued them to the Freikorps in their struggle against the Spartacists in what amounted to a civil war. Here a female tank named *Hanni* is crunching its way over a rather ineffective barricade in Berlin in March 1919. Once the Germans surrendered in the summer of that year these tanks were all supposed to be scrapped.

ANTI-TANK – David Willey

German responses to defeating the tank went through a series of phases – urgency followed by declining concern, followed again, after Cambrai, by a renewed urgency – and took a number of forms ranging from grenades, tank traps and blocks, new artillery tactics, new anti-tank weapons or conversions and improvements to existing weapons, mines and flamethrowers.

The appearance of tanks on the Somme battlefield for the first time in September 1916 was a genuine surprise to the Germans and created in some places *tankschreck* (or 'tank horror'). After the initial confused reports from the front line had been analysed and assessed, the German High Command responded by ordering their own tank and more urgently created 50 batteries of 'close-combat' artillery numbered from 201 to 250.

After experiments the German Army decided that gun calibres of 57mm to 77mm were needed to defeat tanks. In early 1917 a new anti-tank round was developed for the 77mm gun by Krupp that could penetrate 30mm of armour at 3,000m.

The new artillery units were issued with the 77mm field cannon 96 n.A. but with smaller wheels than on the standard gun (1m diameter as opposed to the usual 1.36m diameter). These batteries had no ammunition limbers and had only four horses to pull each gun instead of six. This was because the new batteries were ordered to certain areas of the front line and the guns dug into pits and hidden. The guns were to remain there and not take part in standard artillery engagements such as bombardments and counter-battery work. They were only to be wheeled from their disguised positions to engage with the enemy when attacked by infantry or tanks. Defeating a tank brought monetary rewards – 500 marks were offered for a tank kill compared to just 150 for bringing down an aeroplane.

Other methods

The German Army had armour-piercing bullets in service before the tank appeared on the battlefield. These SmK 7.92mm fitted the normal rifles and machine guns

with a chrome nickel-steel core and were designed to penetrate armoured shields used on observation points or by snipers in the trenches. The bullets, however, were difficult to manufacture and never available in the quantities required.

Grenades were sometimes used as demolition or concentrated charges (*Gelballte Ladung*) and two extra heads wired to a normal grenade was also used to disable tracks or penetrate roofs. Photographs show some clusters with up to eight heads strapped to a single grenade. The chicken-wire netting seen on the Mark I tanks was put in place in anticipation of thrown grenades lodging on the flat roof. Improvisations using

ABOVE The Graincourt gun. The 77mm field cannon 96 n.A was the standard German artillery piece of the war. This particular gun hit several tanks of the 7th Battalion Tank Corps at Graincourt on 20 November 1917 before it was silenced by Gorgonzola II, commanded by Lieutenant A.G. Baker, MC (left), and Gunner D.T. Philip, MM. The gun was recovered as a trophy.

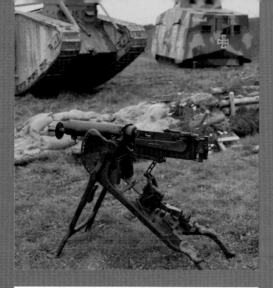

RIGHT The MG 08 and the later MG 08/15 could both fire the standard 7.92mm S.m.K. armour piercing ammunition, but this was always in limited supply. The MG 08 with the *Schlittern* or sledge mount (shown here), was a weighty combination (52kg) so a lighter version of the gun was produced.

RIGHT The MG 08/15 was considerably lighter at 15kg than the standard earlier model. It was designed to be a more portable weapon with a simple bipod to rest on. This example was captured by the Tank Corps on 24 November 1917 during the Cambrai battle.

RIGHT The 77mm *K-Flakwagen*. Its mobility was restricted to roads but with the new armour piercing round it was a potent anti-tank weapon.

RIGHT An experimental half-track vehicle made by Daimler in late 1918. Fitted with a 37mm naval gun the vehicle was designed to provide more cross-country flexibility than the wheeled *K-Flakwagen*.

similar materials continue to be made on armoured vehicles to this day.

The Germans realised that the K-Flak mobile anti-aircraft batteries could also be used against tanks. The vehicles were made by two manufacturing teams, Krupp and Daimler and Ehrhardt and Rheinmetall, based on a requirement for an 80hp four-wheel-drive vehicle for anti-balloon and aircraft defence. These mainly 77mm anti-aircraft guns, mounted openly on the rear of the trucks, had a fast rate of fire. They were issued with new armour-piercing ammunition, the K Granate 15 P. Their mobility meant they could be quickly brought to an area, as seen at the Battle of Cambrai. The vehicle's success led to other experiments with weapons mounted on trucks and half-tracked vehicles before the end of the war.

Special supports were made for the 7.58cm *Minenwerfer* or mine thrower to allow the weapon to be used in an anti-tank role. This small light mortar with a rifled barrel had previously been used in the front line with wheels that could be quickly attached to allow it to be dragged forward to accompany an infantry attack. The new mount added an extended trail, more like an artillery gun, which allowed rounds to be fired directly – on a flat trajectory – at a target up to 1,200m with a 4.6kg round.

'Tankforts' were also designed to be built in areas thought susceptible to tank attack. These could be permanent concrete placements for anti-tank weapons of various calibres or mobile armour-plated pillboxes called a 'Panzerkuppel'. These housed a 5.7cm quick-firing gun and could be moved into position on a special carriage.

A considerable number of photographs exist and are often reproduced showing German soldiers training with flame-throwers as an anti-tank weapon. The *Flammenwerfer* came in a number of sizes:

- The 'Grof' was the largest, a static system that held 100 litres of oil which could propel flame out to 45m for a 1-minute duration.
- The 'Klief' was a man-portable cylinder that carried 10 litres of oil and a lower section compressed gas to project the oil. A second operator held the hose that projected the flame up to 29m for a 5-second duration.
- The 'Wex' was the more familiar double doughnut-shaped backpack with the outer ring carrying the oil and the inner the compressed gas. One man could carry and operate this system, jetting flame up to 18m.

All these systems meant troops had to wait until a tank was remarkably close before operation.

Traps and blocks

One of the simplest ways to disable an

approaching tank was to dig a pit to trap it. Pits or traps were hidden with covering nets or branches and turf: 4m deep by 4m wide was considered ideal. Sometimes mines were placed at the bottom of the pits or they were filled with water to drown the engine. The width of trenches was also considered and the High Command thought 2.5m-wide trenches would prove an obstacle to tanks crossing without assistance.

On roads, concrete blocks were positioned or logs or girders sunk into the road to form a barrier. Near Verdun the Germans threaded steel cable between blocks to create a heavy-duty fence line to protect against tanks.

Initially the Germans improvised mines from existing ammunition such as artillery shells or mortar rounds. These were placed in the ground, sometimes covered with a board or plank to increase the pressure area. The usual fuse was replaced by a Druckzunder or pressure fuse. Generally a charge of 12 to 25kg was needed to effectively destroy a tank.

The urgency to find methods to defeat tanks lessened in 1917 as the Germans saw failed tank attacks at Arras and Bullecourt. Here mud and shellfire meant the tanks had little immediate impact on the course of the battles. During these spring conflicts a number of training tanks, including D26, a Mark II male, were pressed into the fray (another such tank that saw action at this time, *Flying Scotsman*, now resides in the Tank Museum). A training tank had 'soft' steel plates, not heat-treated armour plate. D26 was knocked out in German-held territory and was subsequently inspected and photographed by the enemy. As their standard SmK ammunition had easily penetrated the armour (the Germans not knowing this was an unarmoured training tank) and other tanks had been disabled by shellfire, the German High Command relaxed their own anti-tank activities and tank-making programme. The first use of French tanks in April in the Chemin des Dames only reinforced the German confidence as Schneider vehicles suffered high losses. Lulled into a false sense of security, in May 1917 the new special artillery batteries were disbanded.

Despite the use of Mark IV tanks in

Flanders later in the year and the capture of an example, the German Army failed to realise the armour was thicker and generally bulletproof against standard rifle and SmK ammunition.

The initial success of the tanks at Cambrai in November 1917 reawoke the German High Command to the potency of the new weapon. Captured Mark IV vehicles were assembled to be reused by new German tank units. The A7V (Allegmeine Kreigs-Department 7 Abteilung Verkehrswesen or General War Department 7, Traffic Section) was designed by Joseph Vollmer (1871–1955) in early 1917. After the First World War Vollmer went on to work in Czechoslovakia and Sweden and is perhaps one of the great 'unknowns' of tank development. The A7V chassis were constructed first, but the lessening threat of Allied tanks meant the tank-building programme dropped in priority. Only after Cambrai was armour plate made available for the completion of the first ten A7Vs in December 1917. They were used in combat in March 1918 and the first tank versus tank engagement took place at Villers-Bretonneux in April. The anti-tank capability of the vehicle had few practical opportunities to demonstrate its potential in the First World War.

The German Army Headquarters had ordered a new anti-tank rifle in October 1917. The successes of the tanks at Cambrai speeded up production but the new Tankgewehr rifle did not see widespread use until much later in 1918. The gun was a 13mm single-shot rifle of impressive size. Some 15,800 of the guns had been made by the Armistice but they were not popular with the troops. The recoil was considerable and even with a well-aimed and successfully penetrating shot a tank might still not be disabled as the small round might not hit a critical component. This problem was amply demonstrated at a test in September 1918 when 18 rounds were fired at a captured Mark IV, none of which were thought to have effectively knocked the tank out.

A high number of other anti-tank weapons were being tested in 1918 for potential production and use in 1919, including a machine gun to fire the 13mm rounds of the Tankgewehr. However, the defeat of the German armies in the latter half of 1918 and the Treaty of Versailles brought an end to these developments.

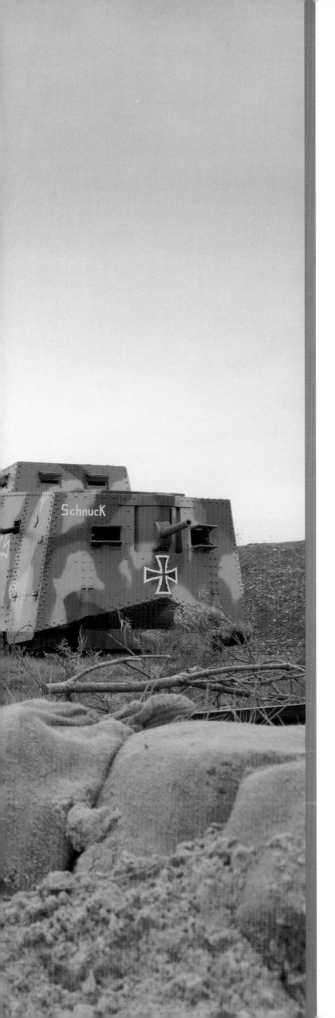

Chapter Seven

Retirement and survivors

There are probably seven or eight original Mark IV tanks left in the world today. Out of 1,200 that is not very many. Five have been chosen for this chapter for the interesting stories they can tell, giving the reader an appreciation of how and where they were made, their varied experiences in war, and what led to their preservation. However, these survivors will have to last forever in as original condition as possible, which presents problems for those charged with their preservation.

OPPOSITE The replica Mark IV and A7V tanks in the Tank Museum's arena. The use of replicas will inevitably increase as the risk of damage by running of real First World War vehicles becomes too great.

129

RETIREMENT AND SURVIVORS

ABOVE A Mark IV female tank operated as a tourist attraction at Southend-on-Sea by a consortium of retired Tank Corps officers after the First World War.

BELOW Named *Whiskey & Soda*, this Mark IV male tank is pictured in Ireland towards the end of the war. Notice that it is not fitted with un-ditching beam rails, probably because it does not need them.

Survivors

An early edition of the *Tank Corps Journal* issued shortly after the First World War invited retired Tank Corps officers to become involved in an unspecified scheme. This turned out to be a novelty tourist attraction using a pair of redundant Mark IV tanks adapted to give rides to holidaymakers at Southend-on-Sea, then a very popular resort east of London.

Photographs show a Mark IV tank, with its sponsons removed but fitted with a large, overhanging upper deck with seats for passengers. An artist's impression in a popular magazine also shows a lower deck in the form of seats, facing forwards, in the narrow gangway either side of the engine. Some film footage also exists, showing one of these modified tanks on the move, complete with apparently happy upper-deck passengers, but

how long the scheme lasted and what a typical trip involved is not recorded. As a business venture one suspects that it was short-lived.

At least two Mark IV tanks are known to have been stationed in Ireland around 1918. Named respectively *Scotch & Soda* and *Whiskey & Soda* (the latter in Cork), how useful they were in an internal security role and whether their crews were drawn from the Tank Corps is not known. From January 1919 control of these tanks and others came under 17th (Armoured Car) Battalion Tank Corps and the Mark IV machines were replaced by Mark V* and Medium A Whippet tanks.

In addition to the fund-raising tank HMLS *Britannia*, a dozen Mark IV female tanks were supplied to the United States Army, one of which survives in the Ordnance Museum in Maryland. Quite why they wanted these obsolete tanks is not clear; they had operated Mark V tanks during the war and obtained Mark V* tanks soon afterwards.

Single tanks were sent to Australia and Canada for fund-raising purposes, both of which are preserved. However, a plan to supply a Mark IV to the Federated Malay States appears to have been abandoned. The Malay States supplied funds sufficient for two tanks, one of which was decorated with Eyes and fitted with an engraved plate; it saw service in France with 6th Battalion. According to Albert Stern it was hoped that it would be donated to the Malay States after the war, but there is no evidence that this ever happened.

The Japanese acquired one Mark IV female tank after the war, along with some Medium A Whippets and other surplus war material. Evidence seems to show that these were used both to inform Japanese engineers on current technology and provide the Japanese Army with a range of vehicles with which to work out their tactical options. The Mark IV was probably their least useful acquisition and its ultimate fate is not known.

A Mark IV female was used for some time at the Royal Naval Air Station at Pulham in Norfolk. A pyramid-shaped tower was fitted to the top to which the nose of an airship could be anchored and moved around by the tank; the idea seems to have been to replace the large, human, ground-handling party, although how contact

ABOVE A female Mark IV engaged in fundraising in the United States. It is seen performing one of the popular stunts that it was capable of, wrecking a large wooden building.

ABOVE Fosters-built Mark IV male tank, No 2341, was given the name Fan-Tan for the Cambrai battle. It was built from monies raised by the Federated Malay States, facilitated by Mr Eu Tong Sen, and was decorated with a pair of Chinese eyes at the front, in keeping with a Chinese tradition applied to trading junks and other vessels.

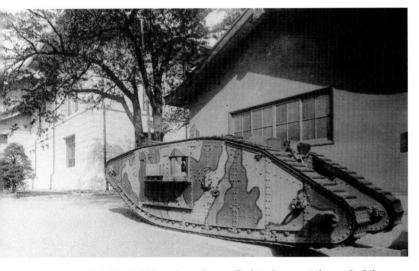

ABOVE A Mark IV female tank supplied to Japan at the end of the war. Finished in an exotic camouflage scheme it appears to have had no influence on subsequent Japanese tank design.

ABOVE Mark IV female, training No 261, which was used for airship handling at the Royal Naval Airship Station, Pulham, Norfolk. It was fitted with a light steel tower to which the airship could be attached, but how one communicated with the tank crew for this delicate operation is not clear.

LEFT A Mark IV female fitted with anti-mine rollers at Dollis Hill in North London. The experiment, initiated by Admiral Sir Reginald Bacon, used two Invicta rollers, from Aveling and Porter steam rollers, but was not successful.

ABOVE The same tank, still at Dollis Hill but being used here as a dead-weight, towed by the prototype Whippet tank. The sponson apertures have been blanked off by wooden shutters.

ABOVE A Mark IV Supply Tank used at Bovington Camp. It is fitted with the usual salvage jib but also, in this case, a large manually operated winch on a platform at the back, making it a useful crane tank.

was maintained between the airship and the tank is unclear.

There is also an unconfirmed report that a Mark IV tank was used by Lieutenant Colonel Philip Johnson in his quest to develop a high-speed tank. This report mentions a Mark IV tank provided with heavy-duty leaf springs to give an improved ride, but whether Johnson also fitted a more powerful engine and improved transmission is not known. A photograph also exists of a Mark IV female tank fitted with a pair of heavy-duty rollers that appear to be taken from two municipal steam rollers. They are believed to be part of a scheme to detonate mines, created at the Mechanical Warfare Department's Experimental station at Dollis Hill. The project appears to have been initiated by Admiral Sir Reginald Bacon, the Controller of Munitions Inventions, but no report of trials can be traced.

The Ashford tank

Stories about the tank on display at Ashford in Kent are few, since its identity is unclear, but the odds are that it spent its working life as a training tank either for driving and maintenance at Bovington or gunnery training at Lulworth. The large, three-digit number on each side indicates that it is a Mark IV female tank, although one can tell this simply by looking at it. Its ultimate fate is another indication. However, it does serve as an introduction to another aspect of the Mark IV tank story.

Two Mark IV tanks, one male, one female, participated in the Lord Mayor's Show through the streets of the City of London in November 1917. This proved to be so popular that a Mark IV male machine was included in an exhibition of war weapons in Trafalgar Square at about the same time; and the subsequent success of the Battle of Cambrai, which was celebrated by a flamboyant ringing of church bells throughout London, must have enhanced this appreciation of tanks.

As a result five male Mark IV tanks were nominated as Touring Tanks under the auspices of the National War Savings Committee and this included the tank that had been on display in Trafalgar Square which, for touring purposes, now bore the name *Nelson* for obvious reasons, although it still sported its training number 130. The other Touring Tanks were 113 *Julian*, 138 *Iron Ration*, 137 *Drake* and 119 *Old Bill*, later joined by the battle-damaged fighting tank *Egbert*. Their role was to tour the country by rail, visiting towns and cities in England, Wales and Scotland (although Scotland operated its own fund-raising scheme). At each location the tank was unloaded from the train, had its male sponsons extended to fighting trim and was then driven by its skeleton crew to a prominent location. Here it served as a platform from where local civic dignitaries could make suitably patriotic speeches and as a focal point for the sale of redeemable War (and subsequently, Victory) Bonds. This usually involved a pretty girl

ABOVE Male and female Mark IV tanks took part in the procession as part of the Lord Mayor's Show in the City of London on 1 November 1917.

ABOVE *Nelson*, the Trafalgar Square tank, with its crew. The character on the left was a civilian who liked wearing uniform and helping with the tank.

from a local bank sitting in one of the sponsons dishing out savings certificates, which were then paid for over the counter at a nearby bank or post office. The sums raised at these events were quite substantial, even by modern standards, and might best be described as an investment in victory, encouraged by the presence of the tank.

In 1919 the National War Savings Committee, with the agreement and cooperation of the War Office, earmarked some 265 tanks for distribution to communities throughout England and Wales that had raised above a certain amount per head of population. The tanks, mostly training machines from Bovington, were taken to the township in question by rail and then driven to a selected location, either a public park or square, and parked up, invariably on a plinth that had been prepared for the occasion. Here local dignitaries would again make speeches while the officer in charge of the tank would regale the crowd with an anecdote about this particular tank's wartime record, although this was invariably fictitious since the tank in question had probably never been abroad.

At first it was decided that tanks supplied in this way should preferably be female machines, partly because the type was more numerous but also because, without armament, the tank was less of a threat to established authority at a time when revolutionary feelings were believed to be running high. Some male machines were

distributed, mostly to locations associated with the development of the tank or with the personalities involved, and subsequently male tanks were distributed to other locations, often those that were added to the list (Chiswick for example) when one of those originally selected dropped out. Some communities rejected the offer, either because they could not find anywhere to put the tank or on moral grounds. And it has to be said that generally speaking the static tanks were not popular in their communities and the majority had been removed and scrapped by 1939. The remainder vanished during the Second World War, all bar one – the Ashford Tank.

A rare survivor, this tank was delivered by rail to the South Eastern and Chatham Railway station in Ashford on Friday 1 August 1919, and a procession was organised, headed by the

BELOW Touring tank *Old Bill* on tour. The railway loading gauge reminds us why the tank's male sponsons had to be squeezed inboard when travelling by rail.

LEFT Crowds gather to watch the arrival of the Ashford tank. Beyond the fact that it carried training number 245, this female example is totally anonymous.

town band, to escort the tank through the town streets to where a plinth had been prepared for it on a traffic island in St George's Square.

The officer in charge of the tank was a Captain Farrar, MC, presumed to be the previously mentioned Walter Frederick Farrar of F (or 6th) Battalion, who had been awarded a Military Cross when his *Flying Fox II* tank plunged off a bridge at Masnières into the St Quentin Canal during the Battle of Cambrai (see Chapter 6). In the original Royal Tank Regiment history this event is attributed to an officer named Edmonds but the citation, in *The Tank Corps Book of Honour*, clearly names Farrar as the officer involved.

Once the tank had been installed on its plinth, Farrar told the crowd that this particular tank had seen service in France and fought at Arras, Vimy Ridge and Cambrai, although the number 245, which was visible on the tank when it arrived, suggests that it was only ever a training machine, probably based at Bovington. Once the presentation ceremony was over, as guests of honour the crew were treated to a recital by the Ashford Town Band after which, following normal practice, the tank was disabled by removing the final drive chains and the crew set off back to Bovington.

The reason why the Ashford tank has survived over many other presentation tanks that went for scrap over the years, is probably due to the fact that the South Eastern Electricity Board installed an electricity substation in the back of the tank, replacing the hull fittings and petrol tank by a pair of rear doors. Since this made it something more useful than an ornament, the tank was retained on its rapidly overgrown island, close by the Old Prince of Wales pub. However the electrical equipment had been removed by 1972 and for a while the tank went into a period of decline.

By 1982, when the area was being

ABOVE Lieutenant Walter Farrar's own tank, F22, *Flying Fox II*, ended up at the bottom of the St Quentin Canal at Masnières during the Cambrai battle. Subsequently, the Germans erected a temporary bridge above it.

LEFT The Ashford tank as many will remember it in the 1960s, the only one of its kind to survive but already deteriorating.

redeveloped, the Ashford tank had generated a certain amount of fame, with interest from Lincoln, Bovington and Canada, so it was decided to clean it up and place a weatherproof cover over it. The redevelopment involved creating a new pedestrian shopping mall that incorporated St George's Square, and the tank which, at around the same time was adopted by the local branch of the Royal Tank Regiment Association, was smartened up and repainted, with the training number '245' on the front, although the white/red/white stripes and the number 'T1234' are entirely spurious. It now resides on its concrete plinth beneath a substantial roof supported by six stout columns.

In 2005 more work was done on the tank at a cost, quoted in the *Ashford Voice*, as costing £12,500, which involved rebuilding the rear end. On Armistice Day (11 November) 2006 the tank was formally dedicated as a war memorial.

Lodestar III, 4093

*L*odestar III can be seen in the Musée Royale de l'Armee in Brussels and it has been chosen for two reasons. First, it is a male tank like the Tank Museum's *Excellent*, built by Sir W.G. Armstrong Whitworth & Co. Ltd of Newcastle upon Tyne, as may be judged by its number 4093, and it is a war veteran, having

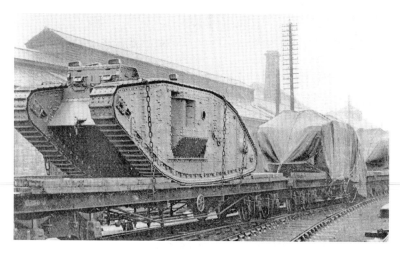

seen active service in France. Second, *Lodestar III* served with 12th (or L) Battalion, one of two Tank Corps battalions to retain Mark IV tanks through to the end of the war – the other was the 7th (or G) Battalion.

The Mark IV tank order that included *Lodestar III* – placed in December 1916, but final drawings only completed on 7 January 1917 – was for 100 tanks, probably all male, which were assembled in Armstrong Whitworth's Close Works in Gateshead.

The 12th Battalion was formed at Bovington in July 1917, composed mostly of men drawn from the Machine Gun Corps Cavalry Depot at Uckfield in Sussex and was commanded by Lieutenant Colonel A.G. McClintock. It moved to Southampton on 2 January 1918 and landed in Le Havre three days later, but without tanks at this time. In France 12th Battalion, in company

with 7th and 11th Battalions was formed into the new 4th Tank Battalion, but from March they were issued with Lewis guns and sent into the line with the infantry.

Although the battalion was issued with Mark IV tanks on arrival in France they subsequently went to Merlimont on the coast, believing that they would now be trained on Mark V tanks, or possibly even Whippets. In the event, since both types were in short supply they reverted to the Mark IV again and their War Diary has quite a lot to say about the poor condition some of these tanks were in.

The battalion was in action at Moyenneville on 21 August during what is more commonly known as the Battle of Bapaume. This was part of the sequel to the Battle of Amiens whereby Haig elected to keep the enemy off balance by striking forcefully in different locations over a period of time. The Battalion War Diary recounts how mist confused navigation and records that even though the 15th Battalion, equipped with Mark V tanks, had moved in around mid-morning to take over the pursuit, it was noon before the stragglers had been rounded up and the battalion was complete again.

Bearing in mind that 12th Battalion did not arrive in France until January 1918, it might seem surprising that a named tank such as *Lodestar* had graduated to a third manifestation in such a short time. Unfortunately neither the Battalion War Diary, nor the War History identify individual tanks very often, so all we know for

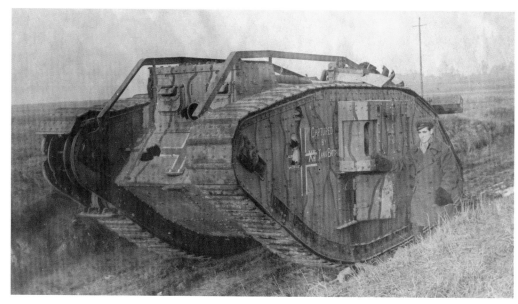

certain is that there was a tank named *Lodestar* – a male tank – numbered 8081, so we can account for at least two of these incarnations.

The battalion was originally issued with Mark IV tanks in time for the German offensive in March and April 1918 but these were later handed in when told they would be converted to operating Whippet tanks. However, events caught up with them – drawing 42 Mark IV tanks in time for the Battle of Amiens in August 1918 – and they never became a Whippet battalion. The tanks they acquired were not new, although maybe new to them, and rumour had it that quite a few of them had taken part in the Cambrai battle of 1917. Now, though, they had all been repaired and were absorbed into 12th Battalion, taking their names and company numbers. This may well have included *Lodestar II*. From then until the end of October the battalion was in more or less constant action. Tanks lost would have been replaced, so a *Lodestar III* entering service towards the end of the battalion's active life could well be possible at this time, and if the crew survived it was quite normal for them to name their new tank after their old one, adding II or even III as appropriate.

There is no hard evidence to indicate whether *Lodestar III* actually saw combat action or not, and while it is fitted with items that suggest that it was equipped to carry and launch a crib, this may have been the standard arrangement for a lot of tanks at this time and certainly does not prove a definite role in battle.

HMS Excellent

HMS *Excellent* was a three-decker, line-of-battle, ship, which was anchored in Portsmouth Harbour in 1830. Under the care of Commander George Smith, RN, it served as a gunnery school for officers and men of the Royal Navy. She lay somewhat to the north of the present dockyard, close to what was known as Whale Island, on a bearing that allowed her to fire her guns across the acres of shallow water and mud flats that comprised a lot of the northern part of the harbour where the risk of danger or damage was minimised.

Whale Island was then little more than an uninhabitable mudbank, adjacent to an even smaller mudbank known as Little Whale Island. By 1867, when new docks were being dug at Portsmouth, the spoil was used to infill the area between the two islands until one large island was created, referred to only as Whale Island. To begin with this was used as a rifle range but in due course buildings started to appear. At its largest the island covered about 72 acres and it was connected to the mainland at Stamshaw by a causeway and lifting bridge. By this time an earlier rail connection, across a viaduct to the dockyard, had been dismantled.

Among the officers associated with Whale Island, or HMS *Excellent* as it had now become with the decommissioning of the warship, was Captain Percy Moreton Scott, who commanded HMS *Excellent* between 1903 and 1905. As one of the Royal Navy's foremost gunnery experts he had considerable faith in Whale Island and probably did more to improve the facilities there than any other commander before or since. Scott was instrumental in establishing the reinforced mudbank by improving drainage, planting grass and trees and laying down roadways. Incidentally, when King Edward VII visited Whale Island in February 1904 Scott laid on a mock battle with his own Wolseley motor car, fitted with a Maxim machine gun to represent an armoured car, long before such things were even being considered by the British Army.

From about 1917, as the Heavy Branch and later the Tank Corps expanded, something approaching 2,000 men were trained at Whale Island on the six-pounder Hotchkiss gun until the Tank Corps set up its own establishment at Lulworth. As a result it was decided by the War Office that HMS *Excellent* should be presented with a tank, a male one since it mounted the same guns. It arrived on 29 March 1919, driving across the causeway from the mainland, and an official handing-over ceremony was arranged for 1 May, just a month later. The Tank Corps party was headed by Brigadier General E.B. Mathew-Lannowe, commanding the Tank Corps Training Centre at Bovington, and it was received by Captain Robert Bax, RN, officer commanding HMS *Excellent*. For the record a tank was also presented to HMS *Pembroke* at Chatham Dockyard where more Tank Corps gunners had been trained, at the Naval School

RIGHT Presentation of 2324 to HMS *Excellent* at Whale Island on 1 May 1919. Colonel E.B. Matthew-Lannowe stands on the platform in front of the tank, with a Tank Corps guard of honour to the left.

of Gunnery. However, the type of tank involved is not known and unfortunately did not survive.

The tank presented to Whale Island was one of those built by William Foster & Co. of Lincoln, number 2324 but bearing the training number 102 on each side so it was always referred to at the time as Tank 102. It would probably be more correct to say that the tank was assembled at Foster's, since the term 'built' suggests a start to finish process, which was certainly not the case here. For example, the main mechanical parts – the engine, clutch, gearbox and differential, plus the radiator – were delivered from the Daimler Company at Coventry, the sponsons were put together by Clayton & Shuttleworth, also of Lincoln, while the weapons arrived from state-controlled institutions such as the Royal Ordnance Factories.

ABOVE A view inside Foster's tank assembly shed with Mark IV tanks being prepared. The overhead crane at the far end would be used to lower the engine assembly on its subframe through the roof of the tank, but in the main it was very labour-intensive work.

RIGHT Female members of Foster's staff pose alongside a Mark IV male at the Wellington Foundry.

The situation with regard to the main hull plates is less clear, at least where Foster's is concerned. It has been suggested that they were delivered, ready assembled up to a point, from one of the Metropolitan group factories in the Birmingham area, but this cannot be confirmed and in any case it was by no means the start of the process. According to information supplied by the English Steel Corporation in 1967, armour plate for British tanks in the First World War was a nickel chromium steel compound equivalent, in its armoured form, to a more modern Izod Test figure of 100, which is not much different to the figure quoted for British light armoured vehicles in the Second World War. The Izod Test essentially measures the toughness of armour by testing it to breaking point.

One drawback of tough armour like this was that it could not be cut or drilled once it had been treated, so this had to be done before it went through the armouring, or hardening, process. This involved heating the plate to about 200 degrees centigrade and then cooling it rapidly in a press filled with cold water so that, in theory at least, the plate was unable to warp or crack. Much of this work was undertaken by William Beardmore & Co. of Glasgow, but as tank production expanded more firms in Britain were drawn into the programme.

Thus the component parts of the hull – that is, the track frames, front and rear panels, floor and roof – would be delivered to the erectors who then riveted them up, using shafts passing through various openings in the frame to align them. The partly assembled hull would then be passed on to the final assembler, such as Foster's, to emerge in due course as a complete, running tank. The frames to which the armour plates were riveted seem to have come from other steel producers, although these parts had not undergone the armouring process.

Not all of the panels were riveted in place; some were bolted so that internal components could be accessed for replacement and repair and, of course, some could not be fitted at all until the parts were installed in the factory. Other contractors seem to have supplied track links, sprocket gears, driving chains, machine-gun mountings and so on, from which it would appear that the task of the major contractors

was final assembly. The official history of the Ministry of Munitions refer to these as erectors, probably a much more accurate term.

Late in 1940, while the threat of a German invasion was still considerable, Second Lieutenant Alec Menhinick of the Royal Army Service Corps, was posted back to Whale Island where he had previously served in charge of a battery of lorry-mounted four-inch guns. Now at a loose end until further orders came through, Menhinick decided to try to revive the old Mark IV tank, which had been there since 1919, and add it to the local defences. Some parts had rusted away and had to be remanufactured, while others were removed, with the Mayor's permission, from the city's own presentation tank that was parked on a concrete base on the edge of Southsea Common, having also been delivered in 1919. The Portsmouth tank was broken up for the war effort shortly after this.

Menhinick not only got the old tank running, he replaced the regular roof hatch with a drum-shaped cupola, mounted a Lewis gun, flew a large white ensign from the back and, with himself in command, took the tank for its first run ashore to a pub called the Air Balloon on Portsea Island. Here both the tank and crew were refreshed before heading back across the causeway to Whale Island, during which they reportedly wrecked a parked car, the property of a commercial traveller. Legend has it that,

BELOW When first restored to running order early in the Second World War, *Excellent* seems to have run without its main armament. Here it is returning to Whale Island across the causeway from Portsmouth.

RIGHT Tank 2324, *Excellent*, as restored and modified by Alec Menhinick, complete with Lewis gun mounting, white ensign and camouflage paint.

as a result, the tank was banned from further excursions, but there is some evidence that it also made a number of trips from Whale Island to the playground at Northern Parade School, between Doyle Avenue and Kipling Road in Portsmouth which, during the war, served as an annexe to HMS *Excellent*, providing dormitory facilities for personnel posted to the naval establishment.

While stories such as this can breed myths, it does seem safe to say that this was the only Mark IV tank to see any kind of active service in the Second World War. Menhinick claimed that although they did not engage enemy aircraft with the Lewis gun, it was used to bring down parachute flares quite successfully. Had the Germans managed to effect a landing in the Portsmouth area, a restored First World War tank would probably have been the least of their worries.

Towards the end of the war the tank was put out to grass, almost literally, alongside a road in a quiet corner of Whale Island behind a low security fence and among grass that threatened to grow up and submerge it. At this time the six-pounder guns seem to have been removed and the apertures in the sponsons plated over, although the Lewis gun cupola was retained.

Starting in 1969 attempts were made to restore the tank to its original condition, but work seems to have progressed in fits and starts.

ABOVE The tank after a run ashore, outside the ornate gates to Whale Island. Menhinick is near the back of the tank to the left of the naval officer.

RIGHT Members of the Royal Naval party who undertook the restoration of the tank; with the tracks removed one can see the skid rails and return rollers.

BELOW Looking to the rear one can see the rear door, additional ammunition stowage and the rear extension of the engine bearers. The large oval hole is covered externally by a louvred panel, and the two smaller holes are connected to the filler and draining point for the radiator.

RIGHT The gutted hull looking forwards, showing the ammunition stowage and main engine bearers.

ABOVE LEFT This photograph shows the tank inside 18 Command Workshops, REME, at Bovington with the differential and gearbox assembly being lowered into place.

ABOVE Fully restored *Excellent* rolls out of 18 Command Workshops in 1975. Next stage, the return handover ceremony.

From early 1970 it was undertaken by serving personnel from HMS *Excellent* under Lieutenant D.A. Ward. Much of the interior of the tank was stripped out, cleaned and repainted, although some items, notably those connected with the water-cooling system such as the radiator and fan, were too far gone with rust and had to be replaced. By 1975 the tank had been removed to the Lymington engineering firm of Wellworthy Ltd and from there to 18 Command Workshops, Royal Electrical and Mechanical Engineers at Bovington, where it was prepared and a crew trained to drive it for the final handover ceremony at the Tank Museum on 29 May 1975. For some odd reason the balls in the machine-gun mounts in each sponson were the modified type designed to accept the Hotchkiss gun, while that in the front of the cab still had a ball capable of holding a Lewis gun, but when this was done is not entirely clear.

In the summer of 1984 the tank was again

ABOVE On 29 May 1975 *Excellent* was handed back to the Tank Museum. The group included senior naval and military personnel, a crew for the tank in period uniforms, two nurses in period uniforms and the Tank Museum curator – at the time, the late Colonel Peter H. Hordern, OBE, DSO – on the extreme left.

BELOW Moving off in a cloud of fumes the old tank is followed by a large crowd of visitors.

put into working order to take part in a BBC television series *Soldiers*, narrated by the author Frederick Forsyth. Genuine blank-firing machine guns, two Hotchkiss and one Lewis, were provided and special effects charges used to simulate firing of the main guns. A crew was provided by two members of the museum staff and half –a dozen young soldiers from 1st Royal Tank Regiment.

FLIRT II, F4

*F*lirt II presents a problem since it is not entirely clear whether the tank that fought at Cambrai is the same one currently preserved in Lincoln, but it is worth including as it represents so many aspects of tank history that should be mentioned.

Flirt indicates an F, or 6th Battalion tank and F4 suggests the fourth tank of the first section of the senior company of the battalion. The men who formed the battalion did their initial training at Bovington, which they left on 12 May 1917 under the command of Lieutenant Colonel Frank Summers, DSO, DSC, and sailed for France. They took over their tanks at Wailly, the Tank Corps Driving School near Arras, and saw action for the first time on 31 July 1917 in what

ABOVE During filming for the BBC TV series *Soldiers* in 1984. Film crew and tank crew mingle while they prepare to do static shots.

RIGHT After the filming, *Excellent* – still belching clouds of fumes – makes its way back to the museum.

RIGHT A dramatic photograph, much beloved of book jacket designers, actually shows *Flirt II* on the lip of a mound during its period at Wailly in 1917.

is known to history as the Third Battle of Ypres.

The following brief account, taken from *The War History of the Sixth Tank Battalion* records the activities of F4 on that day; notice that here it is named *Flint*, which may or may not be a misprint, but there is no indication as to whether F4 at this time was a male or a female tank. Nor are any members of the crew named.

F4 '*Flint*'

This Tank proceeded to the Green Line, but arriving late, found the infantry already in possession, and not requiring help. On the return journey the Tank became very badly ditched, near Polizee Wood. As the un-ditching gear had been shot away, the Tank could not then be got out.

The tank currently masquerading as *Flirt II* has been given the number 2179, which appears to be entirely concocted and is probably derived from the fact that it was numbered T179 at the Tank Museum many years ago, which was equally fictitious. As far as can be deduced from recent research no tanks were numbered in the 21** or 22** sequence. Since it is fitted with female sponsons it was probably not built by Foster's, but the tank has undergone at least two major reconstructions in its time – assuming that it is the same tank. This has to be borne in mind when it is being examined for evidence. For example, Richard Pullen, Chairman of the Friends of the Lincoln Tank, discovered the word OLDBURY stamped into one of the hinges of a sponson door, along with the figure M162

embossed on the surface of one of the doors. The door may not originally have been part of this tank, so the significance of its markings is uncertain.

What is known for sure is that a female tank named *Flirt II*, bearing the markings F4, was one of four tanks comprising 16th Company in F (or 6th) Battalion at Cambrai on 20 November 1917.

On the 19th the tanks of 16th and 18th Companies disembarked from the railway at New Heudicourt, just south of the village of

Gouzeaucourt, in readiness for the morning. The area was very congested with the war preparations of others, so it took a while before the tanks could find sufficient space to manoeuvre before moving off. The two companies advanced, heading roughly north-east astride the Gouzeaucourt–Bonavis road with 16th Company on the right. Their first objective was the Blue Line, about four kilometres from Gouzeaucourt, in the first part of the main Hindenburg Line system. *Flirt II* engaged and dispersed German troops before advancing two kilometres towards the second objective, the Brown Line, where it came under fire from two German machine-guns, one of which it located and put out of action. The second gun continued to fire for a while, spattering the armour of the tank and causing splinters to fly around inside, injuring some members of the crew. Having done all that was required of it, *Flirt II* swung around and headed back to the battalion rallying point close to the Blue Line.

As far as is known, every British tank that took part in the attack on the Hindenburg Line at Cambrai on 20 November 1917 carried a fascine on the cab roof, which it dumped into the wider trenches in order to help it and other tanks cross, as described in Chapter 6. Those tanks equipped to carry and launch the fascines had particular attachments that are quite recognisable, and. none of these fittings are visible on the tank now displayed in Lincoln, so some doubt is cast upon the actual identity of this tank, unless such fittings were subsequently removed.

Flirt II was in action again the following day, Wednesday 21 November. The starting point was the small town of Marcoing on the western side of the St Quentin Canal, which meant that all of the tanks – seven from A Battalion and ten from F Battalion – first had to cross the canal by the railway bridge, the only one in the area still standing and capable of taking tanks, before fanning out to assault the Red Line. This was the furthest objective, running across the base of a salient and formed by a sweeping curve in the canal between the village of Rumilly and a location known as Flot Farm.

Flirt II was held up by mechanical problems and did not arrive at the scene of the action until about 13:30hrs, two hours behind the rest of their group. Cooperation with the infantry

was hampered by intense enemy machine-gun fire pouring in from high ground to the west; German machine-gunners were now being issued with armour-piercing bullets for use against tanks so it made the situation more hazardous. *Flirt II* arrived near Flot Farm to find that one tank had become ditched, with another standing by, but were unable to help because incoming machine-gun fire made it virtually impossible for anyone to operate outside a tank. *Flirt II* positioned itself across the bow of the ditched tank to create a bulletproof screen, under cover of which the disabled tank could at last be extracted. One of the male tanks in this group now turned a six-pounder gun on a German strongpoint dug into the railway embankment and further shelling appeared to drive the defenders away.

In the late afternoon, with darkness coming on, *Flirt II* and the other surviving tanks – with crews exhausted – made their way back to the rallying point at Marcoing station on the west side of the canal. *Flirt II* was not involved in further combat, despite substantial actions taking place on the 23rd, and eventually *Flirt*, along with the survivors of F Battalion, were withdrawn to a tank park – known then as Tankodromes – at Ribecourt, well away from the fighting. While there, on two occasions the battalion was notified that tanks would be needed, although in the event they were not required. But it was third time unlucky for *Flirt II*.

Perhaps against his better judgement Field Marshal Haig authorised one last attack, in an effort to recapture Bourlon village on the north-west corner of Bourlon Wood. The attack was to begin before dawn on Tuesday 27 November and the previous day was given over to preparing the tanks and moving them closer to the start line. The assault would be launched by Major General Braithwaite's 62nd Division, supported by 20 tanks – 17 from F Battalion and 3 from C Battalion. The Germans had retaken Bourlon village over the weekend and gone to great efforts to prepare its defence, in particular against tanks.

The plan was for Allied tanks to attack from six different directions, but the Germans had thrown up barricades against them and once they were halted subjected each tank to intense fire from machine guns and anti-tank weapons.

Under this fire *Flirt II* moved into the village, yet was constantly having to stop and turn to avoid wounded men lying on the ground. Close to the village pond *Flirt II* encountered F13, *Falcon II*, which was bogged down in swampy ground with its unditching beam broken. As *Flirt II* tried to manoeuvre clear of F13, all the teeth on the secondary gears were stripped off; the tank became immobilised, as well as partially ditched. Stuck where she was *Flirt II* completely boxed in F13, whose crew were desperately trying to dig her out. At around 08:30hrs tank F1, *Firespite II*, appeared on the scene and managed to tow *Flirt II* clear of F13, although by then neither tank was fit to proceed. An hour or so later German infantry were closing in and *Flirt II* came under sustained machine-gun fire; so much so that it proved impossible for anyone to work outside the tank, and finally the crew decided to abandon it and return on foot, taking their machine guns with them.

Even before the fighting was over, the Germans had teams out on the battlefield, examining abandoned tanks in the areas they controlled, photographing them and ascertaining their value for recovery and restoration. *Flirt II* was one of them, although by then it had been struck at least four times on the port side and, with a liberal covering of mud, looked anything but appealing. Despite this *Flirt II* was earmarked for recovery, because when it was photographed someone had chalked on the side in German: 'Do not remove. Will be towed away. Army HQ'. Some tanks like F13, which only needed digging out, could be driven off, while others had to be hauled away by large tractors, taken to a railhead, jacked up and loaded on to a train for Belgium.

Flirt II's fate in German hands is so closely connected with the issue of other captured tanks that its story can be found in 'Beutepanzers' in Chapter 6, but suffice it to say that there is no evidence to suggest that it was ever restored by the Germans or that its identity could be established at the end of the war. What is known is that a Mark IV female with certain characteristic features was parked on the edge of the Bovington driver training area during the Second World War and in 1949, now named *Flirt II,* arrived at the Tank Museum and was placed on a plinth in front of the building facing King George V Road. All that the curator at the time noted was: 'Tank Mark. IV female "F4" No. T.179. Hull only, no engine etc. inside. 7' x 21'.' Under 'Source' it simply says 'Royal Tank Regiment'.

Assuming that its mechanical parts were removed by German engineers at Monceau-

LEFT Wrecked and abandoned in Bourlon village, *Flirt II* seems to have changed its spots. The device on the nose looks like the four of clubs, yet on earlier pictures it has the four of hearts.

ABOVE The tank that eventually ended up at the Tank Museum purporting to be *Flirt II*, appears in the background of this photograph of a Cromwell on the edge of the driver training area at Bovington, probably towards the end of the Second World War.

LEFT That same tank, now decorated as *Flirt II* but with a totally fictitious number, stood outside the Tank Museum for years with all internal fittings removed and its hull plates cracking, as can be seen.

sur-Sambre, and given the fact that parts of the hull were already damaged, why was it brought back to Britain at all? It was not a tank with an outstanding war record, nor was it an icon of the Cambrai battle such as H1, *Hilda*, would have been; the name of its commander is not even known. If it really is the same tank it must have undergone a cosmetic repair at some stage because plates damaged in Bourlon village were replaced by new ones.

Given that Bovington must have been

LEFT This rear view of *Flirt II* at the Tank Museum shows the wooden panel attached to the side, which seems to identify it. Compare this with the picture with the Cromwell.

swamped with redundant Mark IV tanks at this time, it seems an odd choice to retain one in need of repair and devoid of any internal fittings merely on account of its name. Between 1919 and 1939 it was thought to be on display in a nearby town and was returned to Bovington in preference to it being scrapped, although that is only speculation. At the Tank Museum it stood for the best part of thirty-five years, its original hull panels starting to crack and some track plates being removed to keep others running. Sometime between 1982 and 1984 it was treated with a special rust-proofing substance named Fertan and repainted, but it was clearly in need of major restoration.

In 1984, following negotiations between the Tank Museum and Lincoln City Council, *Flirt II*, or the tank purporting to be *Flirt II*, was lifted off its plinth and transported by road to Lincoln where apprentices and volunteers joined staff at Ruston Gas Turbines Ltd to give the old tank a thorough facelift. Damaged panels were replaced and the interior tidied up, although absent of its interior fittings, which proved impossible to obtain. Once restored the tank spent some time at Royal Air Force Scampton while its future was decided and then, after a short spell at the British Museum, was established as an exhibit at the Museum of Lincolnshire Life, where it may still be seen.

Deborah, D51, 2620

Deborah, battered but recognisable, can be found in a barn in the village of Flesquières, just a short distance from where she was knocked out on 20 November 1917. The tank was identified by a remarkable coincidence shortly after her rediscovery in 1998 when William Heap, grandson of *Deborah's* commander, donated a photograph of the damaged machine in exchange for a copy of his grandfather's Military Cross citation. The photograph revealed identical damage that was later confirmed by a photograph in an old album compiled by Lieutenant Colonel T.L. Wenger, showing *Deborah* in the process of being buried.

Heap's citation reads as follows:

T/2nd Lieut HEAP, FRANK GUSTAVE, 'D' Battn. Awarded MC.

In the Cambrai operations near Flesquières on November 20, 1917, he fought his tank with great gallantry and skill, leading the infantry on to five objectives. He proceeded through the village and engaged a battery of enemy field guns from which his tank received five direct hits, killing four of his crew. Although then behind the German lines he collected the remainder of his crew, and conducted them in good order back to our own lines in spite of heavy machine-gun and sniper fire.

RIGHT Plateau railhead with two trainloads of tanks, complete with fascines, preparing to move off to the final unloading point.

Deborah's original four-digit number identifies it as a tank emanating from the Metropolitan Carriage, Wagon & Finance Company of Birmingham. The tank was almost certainly built by the Oldbury Railway Carriage & Wagon Company of Oldbury, Worcestershire – part of the Metropolitan Group – and was selected as the first company within the group to build tanks, commencing with the Mark I in 1916. *Deborah* was from the second batch of 401 Mark IV tanks ordered from Metropolitan, all of which were female machines.

In the summer of 1917 this tank was shipped over to France and issued to D Battalion Tank Corps, then commanded by Lieutenant Colonel W.F.R. Kyngdon, who would still be in post at Cambrai later in the year. The tank was allotted to 12 Company and issued with the number D51 and the name *Deborah*. Lieutenant George Ranald MacDonald was given its command. With another tank, *Deborah* saw combat on 22 August 1917. The objective was a German strongpoint known as Schuler Farm. The two tanks were waiting to move off from Belle Vue Farm near Poelkapelle when a German barrage came down. One shell struck D51 on a track and MacDonald was severely wounded, putting both tank and commander out of action. In fact three other tanks on the same site were so badly damaged that for the impending skirmish they had to be replaced by tanks and crews from G Battalion.

Deborah could be repaired but it took MacDonald longer to recover so by the time the tank was ready to fight at Cambrai – after some D Battalion training in trench-crossing techniques at Wailly near Arras – a new commander, Second Lieutenant Frank Gustav Heap, had been appointed.

D Battalion arrived at the Plateau railway centre on 14 November where fascines were drawn and fitted. The battalion comprised 35 tanks in all, split between three companies, while each company was divided into four sections; a section of tanks could consist of three or four machines. *Deborah* belonged to No 12 Section, accompanied by D49, *Dollar Princess*, and D50, *Dandy Dinmont*, which was

BELOW Looking along one of the rides that leads into the depths of Havrincourt Wood. Here, on the day before the battle, tanks of D, E and G Battalions hid from German aircraft before setting off for their place on the start line.

ABOVE The ground leading up to Flesquières from Havrincourt does not look all that daunting, but it was enough to hide the advancing tanks from the German guns until it was too late.

the only male tank of the three. The section commander was Captain Graeme Nixon whose service with the tanks went right back to the very start; he commanded D12 at Flers on 15 September 1916 and had always been with the 4th Battalion, even back to its origins as D Company, Heavy Branch, Machine Gun Corps.

From Plateau on 18 November D Battalion were taken to a newly constructed railhead at Ytres on the western edge of the battlefield. Using prepared ramps the 35 tanks climbed down off the train and formed up to drive to their hiding place in the south-eastern corner of Havrincourt Wood. Much of this journey was done in the gathering darkness to avoid detection from the air. Speed was kept to a minimum as the tanks, roughly in line ahead, followed a taped route that took them south, around the straggling village of Neuville Bourjonval, through the northern outskirts of Metz-en-Couture, and always with the dark shadow of Havrincourt Wood looming on their left.

From Metz-en-Couture they swung north-east and, hugging the edge of the wood, made their way into the area that had been set aside for them. Here, according to the Battalion War Diary they were heavily camouflaged against aerial observation, and troops employed to clear the ground of any marks they had made en route to the wood. These would be clearly visible from the air so there was no point in

stringing camouflage nets over the tanks in the wood if the trail they had made getting there was still obvious.

Before dawn on 20 November the tanks were started up, and with engines on tick-over moved slowly along the taped route towards the line from which they would move off to battle. In the case of D Battalion this was just to the east of the small town of Trescault, where they established their headquarters and waited in the pre-dawn light for the signal to move.

BELOW Flesquières photographed from directly overhead about a month before the battle. D51 came to grief on the road leading out of the village to the east.

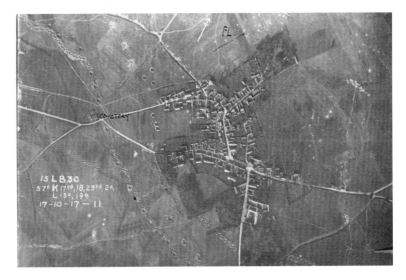

Two companies of other tank battalions would lead the way while a third, setting off about half an hour later, would act as a second wave, passing through the leading group at the first objective, gathering up any surviving tanks and then moving on to the second objective – the prominent village of Flesquières on a low ridge to the north.

Each tank battalion was leading an infantry brigade of the 51st Division, and in the case of D Battalion this was the 153rd Brigade consisting of battalions from the Black Watch and Gordon Highlanders. For some inexplicable reason, the general commanding 51st Division put his own interpretation on his instructions. Major General George Harper did not want his men crowding up behind the tanks so they were held back and deployed differently. As a result they lost contact with their tanks and failed to find those gaps in the wire that the tanks had made.

However, they had a long way to go yet. When the signal gun sounded at 06:20hrs, 10th and 11th Companies moved off, preceded by six tanks given the role of wire crushers. The sector of the line allotted to D Battalion, sandwiched between G Battalion on their left

and E Battalion on their right, was extremely cramped, but this soon resolved itself once the tanks reached the foot of the valley and the first trenches of the Hindenburg Line system. Here the initial trench was probably wider and deeper than anywhere else and only one tank made it across using its fascine; four others tried but failed, seven more developed mechanical trouble, and three turned back due to shortage of supplies.

Deborah and the other tanks of 12th Company were due to move off from the start line at 06:50hrs, but there may have been some confusion since 12th Company commander Major R.O.C Ward was killed, apparently by a stray bullet, just five minutes earlier. He was duly replaced by Captain W. Smith and the tanks got under way. Two of the tanks were temporarily ditched along the route, but in due course they linked up with the survivors of the first wave and led the infantry up the slope towards Flesquières and their first objective, the railway embankment, where D Battalion established a rallying point to which surviving tanks would return after the battle.

Legend and unit pride has blurred events at Flesquières that day, making it difficult to

ABOVE *Deborah*
**damaged and
abandoned in the
street at Flesquières.
It was the pattern
of damage revealed
by this picture that
seemed to prove
conclusively that this
was the tank that had
been found.**

discern the truth, Harper received a lot of the blame for altering the basic plan of attack. It is said that had his soldiers been closer to the tanks they might have saved some of them by firing at the German gunners, but since this is a Tank Corps claim to explain their failure it must be treated with caution. Field Marshal Haig recounted that: 'Many of the hits upon our tanks at Flesquières were obtained by a German artillery officer who, remaining alone at his battery, served a field gun single-handed until killed at his gun. The great bravery of this officer aroused the admiration of all ranks.' This officer was subsequently named as Theodore Kruger who was certainly at Flesquières at this time serving with Artillery Regiment 108. The truth seems to be that the German Army had trained a number of artillery batteries in anti-tank work and elements of two of these were installed on the ridge.

While E Battalion's tanks worked their way around to the east of the village, those from D Battalion edged around to the west. The three tanks from 12th Section had been earmarked to proceed through the village itself. Meanwhile, on the ridge outside Flesquières the German batteries opened up and before long 18 tanks from both battalions lay disabled and, in some cases burning, on the battlefield. Among those tanks knocked out was D49, which was stopped on the edge of the village. Frank Heap's D51, *Deborah*, advanced down

the village street using its Lewis guns to keep enemy heads down. Unfortunately, once it had passed the Germans emerged again and laid down such heavy fire that infantry advancing in the wake of the tank were pinned down and unable to proceed. *Deborah* was on its own. For now, though, it was doing well, protected to some extent by the buildings on each side as it headed through the village towards the second objective, the so-called Brown Line.

Emerging from the edge of the settlement, *Deborah* poked her nose into the open and immediately came under fire from the German guns. Five well-aimed rounds smashed into her, setting her alight and killing or wounding five members of her crew, yet without doing much visible external damage. *Deborah* was finished as a fighting machine but her story was far from over. Frank Heap, largely uninjured but in shock, ushered the survivors out of the tank and escorted them back to safety, which was no mean feat given that Flesquières was still occupied by German troops and British infantry had not yet managed to penetrate the village. This act, one suspects, is what really earned him the award of a Military Cross.

The Germans pulled out of Flesquières overnight and British troops, entering the following morning, discovered the wreck of the tank and the bodies of dead crew members, who were then buried nearby. *Deborah* was too far gone to be recovered, but it is clear that in

LEFT *Deborah* **in the hole where she would remain for the best part of 78 years. The number 51, which finally secured her identification, can be seen on the petrol tank at the back.**

BELOW *Deborah* **rediscovered. The hole in the top has been covered with a panel of corrugated iron. Look at the way the rear horns are turned outwards, which is believed toshow how she was towed backwards.**

due course salvage crews removed many of the more useful mechanical items and the weapons mountings, leaving the hulk where it lay. The Germans ultimately recaptured Flesquières but the wrecked tank was of no interest to them.

The British and Canadians reoccupied the area in September 1918 and during this time *Deborah* seems to have suffered further damage to the front end, although the precise circumstances of this are not clear. Otherwise the tank remained more or less where it had been disabled, up against a building on the edge of the street and so well hidden that it does not show up on any aerial photographs.

Once the fighting was over the task of clearing the battlefields began. Bodies were

exhumed, identified where possible, and reburied in new Commonwealth War Graves Commission cemeteries. Tanks fell into a peculiar category. Some were repaired up to a point and then either driven or towed away. If they were beyond repair they were first stripped of any useful fittings and then blown up. But *Deborah* was rather a special case. While not fit for salvage, with local people gradually returning to the village it was deemed inappropriate to blow it up as collateral damage would be inevitable, due to its resting position. The officer responsible for salvage in this area was Major T.L. Wenger, Tank Corps, and his solution was to bury *Deborah* in an excavation nearby that was part of the German scheme for improving their defences. It was large enough and deep enough to hold a tank so Wenger decided to tow *Deborah* there, using two serviceable tanks. It was dragged backwards to the hole and allowed to fall in. Damage caused by this operation is still visible on the tank.

Monsieur Philippe Gorczynski and fellow enthusiast Jean-Luc Gibot, both Cambrai residents at the time, covered the battlefield for many years, gathering information and relics. Indeed, the outbuildings around Philippe's hotel in Cambrai were rapidly filling with fragments of blown-up tanks, identified where possible and stored on pallets. However, the main prize, that of discovering the remains of a complete tank, eluded them. Rumours abounded and the most persistent centred on the village of Flesquières where one elderly resident, Madame Bouleux, had some confused memories of seeing a tank buried.

Having identified the most likely site an excavator was called in and on 5 November 1998 it uncovered the top hatch of what Philippe Gorczynski was able to identify as a Mark IV female tank. Work continued to uncover the tank, the total unveiling on 20 November 1998 – deliberately arranged by Philippe for that day – coinciding with the 81st

anniversary of the first day of the Battle of Cambrai. In the hole with it was a good deal of battlefield detritus, both British and German. At that time there was no precise indication as to the identity of the tank, but it was already obvious that it had belonged to D Battalion.

Entirely by coincidence, two photographs arrived at the Tank Museum showing a wrecked tank in Flesquières village, and comparisons with the recovered tank soon revealed that they showed the same machine as the damage was identical. On the reverse of one photo was written 'Mr Heap's bus'; there could now be no question – the tank that Jean-Luc and Philippe had discovered was D51, *Deborah*.

The tank was subsequently lifted out of its hole and moved to a building in the village of Flesquières, where it remains at the time of writing.

Running, replicas and responsibilities – David Willey

With the 100th anniversary of the start of the First World War approaching, the desire to see the machinery of the period in motion is obviously strong – especially with something so identifiable with the conflict as the classic rhomboid-shaped tank. However, with only seven known examples of the Mark IV left and just a dozen other tanks of other marks remaining, the Tank Museum has taken the decision not to run its Mark IV, or Mark V (also in working order). The Mark IV was last driven in the 1980s and the Mark V for short distances in the 2000s.

The debates in the heritage sector about running historic machinery continues, the main argument centring around the risk to and loss of originality when machinery is used; parts will inevitably get worn, broken or need replacement. This has to be measured against the interpretive value of seeing machinery operate, allowing the public to see much more of its presence, function, noise, mobility, etc.

Different museums have very different goals and functions and this must be taken into consideration as part of the argument, as should the type of machinery in the collection. The concerns associated with flying a historic

aeroplane, for example, do not just include risks to the important aircraft itself – there is also the pilot and crew to think of. No interpretation is worth the unacceptable risk to life should something go wrong.

There are, of course, many well-reasoned arguments on both sides of the debate and also many questions on how far one might go in the extremes of such discussions. For example, should seeing a weapon of war such as a tank in use include the use of the weaponry, often its primary function? And those who argue against the operation of vehicles often fail to include the practical issue of the continuing operation of parts or sub-systems of even a static item. For instance, suspensions are under load and

ABOVE **With wood to prevent total collapse, the tricky task of lifting** *Deborah* **out of her 'grave' begins.**

BELOW **Broken track plate on the Mark V tank. The structure and resilience of metals changes over time and much more research is needed into how best to conserve 20th century metal machinery like the tank.**

- the known history of any individual vehicle;
- what is identified as significant about this particular example;
- what actions or historical events was it involved in;
- what is original to the vehicle (as with many mechanical items it may have had considerable interventions in its working and heritage life, such as new engines, tracks, paint schemes, etc) and in consequence, what is important to save;
- how complete the item is and what backing and supporting material is available.

bearings will operate if the item is moved. Systems such as hydraulics, lubrication, cooling and fuel will seize, degrade and corrode unless interventions are made.

The Tank Museum now takes a pragmatic and selective approach, treating each vehicle on a case by case basis when the issues and opportunities to deal with them arise. What might be an appropriate response to one vehicle may not be a practical, sensible or ethical response to another. Points to be given attention might include:

As well as these considerations, the vitally important resource implications and requirements of any proposed actions will take a paramount role in the process, as no project should be started without a clear aim in mind and the funding, skills and materials required to meet it.

The Mark V tank at the museum has a number of cracks appearing in the armour plate and a track plate broke across the raised spud during an outing. While the opportunity is always there of replacing the metalwork with new steel, the risk may be that stresses are then increased elsewhere and the slippery slope to the blacksmith's hammer scenario looms ('it's had three new heads and four new handles in its life' – still the same hammer?).

However, the position with the Mark IV and other museum vehicles may change in the future. New technology may mean restoration and conservation activities can be carried out in less intrusive ways. The emphasis and expectations placed on heritage collections may also morph over time and the public may not see the continued merit of publically funded collections that simply 'don't work'. With so much technological and industrial material having been made in the 20th and 21st centuries, museums will have to be incredibly selective as to what can be saved. An increasing weight in choosing may be given to items that can work; looking may not be enough.

In response to the desire to see the rhomboid shape of an operating First World War tank in films, re-enactor events and commemorations, the production of replica vehicles has begun. While some incomplete vehicles were created for stage plays such as *To the Green Fields*, and a fantasy First World War-like tank appeared in the film *League of Extraordinary Gentlemen*, it was Peter Jackson in New Zealand and Steven Spielberg working in the UK who first attempted full-size running replicas of First World War tanks. In Spielberg's version of *Warhorse*, the equine hero of the piece, Joey, meets a tank in the confused horror of the battlefield. Although only on screen for moments, the tank represents modern mechanical warfare, with the horse now seemingly out of place on the battlefield.

By an odd coincidence, the replica tank was made by a company based in the hangars of the old tank experimental site at Chertsey. Here tanks and other military vehicles were developed and tested until the early 2000s when film-makers moved in and the site became known as 'Longcross Studios'. Neil Corbold Special Effects employed a number of military vehicle enthusiasts, so when commissioned to make the replica First World War tank, in many ways it was a labour of love. Visits to the Tank Museum provided the basic measurements for the vehicle's fabrication, built around the engine and running gear of an old Hyundai excavator. A box steel structure was welded together for strength, and mild steel panels and improvisations such as baking trays as the sprocket-tightening housing make the tank look very authentic in design. The weathering of the tank with fake mud and the subsequent running of the vehicle at the museum, has given it a very realistic and used look. When operating, the vehicle seems to slide along the tracks it lays and the slow speed and gentle wobble give a tremendously authentic air, as well as the sheer presence and weight on the ground.

With the 100th anniversary of the war approaching, the Tank Museum had been planning to create a running replica. So the offer of this tank for sale to the museum

after filming was complete in 2010 made the decision to purchase the vehicle an easy one. Subsequently, the replica has been used at Tank Museum events and for use by documentary film-makers.

The tank was joined two years later by another First World War tank replica – this time the German A7V – made by Bob Grundy of British Military Vehicles near Wigan. Construction was started in 2006 and the completed vehicle was shown at Tankfest in 2009. Bob made the tank not for any particular purpose other than his interest in the First World War and to prove he could. These two replicas provide the Tank Museum with a means of showing what the first tanks looked and moved like. In so doing, it is hoped to inspire the public with an interest in the real tanks and their crews.

ABOVE The A7V being displayed at Tankfest in 2009 with re-enactors escorting.

BELOW The Mark IV replica and re-enactors perform at Tankfest 2012 as close infantry support.

Appendix 1

Important early vehicles in the collection of the Tank Museum

The Hornsby Train Track Tractor

Resulting from trials started in 1903 to find a tractor to pull a 16-ton load over 40 miles, the Hornsby was ordered by the War Office in 1909 along with three-wheeled tractors. It had tracks designed by David Roberts but the lack of interest and sales led Hornsby's to sell the design to the American Holt Company. The tractor saw no wartime service but showed that the military were interested in (and aware of) tracks well before the First World War.

Little Willie or No 1 Lincoln Machine

Often referred to as the first tank, this vehicle was the result of the Landships Committee effort to find a viable mechanical method to break the deadlock on the Western Front. Initially, the vehicle had commercially produced tracks, which failed because they dropped away and ran off the vehicle. The designers William Tritton and Walter Wilson had a new design of track made and fitted that proved successful, but they had already designed a more practical vehicle – *Mother*. *Little Willie* therefore, never saw any action.

Mark I Male

This is the sole remaining Mark 1 of the type that first went into action on 15 September 1915. The tank was presented to the Marquess of Salisbury in May 1919 in thanks for allowing the early trials of Little Willie and Mother to take place in his grounds at Hatfield Park. The tank was gifted to the Museum in 1969.

Mark II

(built as a Male – now with a Female sponson)
The Mark II (and Mark III) tanks were built as training tanks and in consequence did not have heat-treated armour plate because they were not destined to go into action. However, the desperate need for tanks on the Western Front saw this Mark II being sent into action at the Battle of Arras in April 1917. It shows damage from German 77mm shellfire at its rear.

Mark IV Male

The main focus of this book. The Mark IV is regularly opened for the visiting public to climb inside at the museum.

Mark V Male

The Mark V could be driven by one man instead of the four needed for the Mark IV. It also had a new engine designed by Harry Riccardo. Four hundred were built, with the first examples seeing action in July 1918. This tank was in action on at least three occasions, the first being at Amiens on 8 August where the commander, Lt Whittenbury, won a Military Cross.

Mark V** Female

When the Germans countered the British tanks by making wider trenches, the tank designers produced a 6ft-longer tank with consequently a better trench crossing capability. The first variant was the Mark V* (an interim solution); the Mark V** was a better design with a troop carrying facility, but the war ended before any saw action. This tank was used by the Royal Engineers at Christchurch to experiment with laying bridges and clearing mines. It therefore became the first armoured engineer vehicle.

Mark VIII

Designed as a cooperative venture in 1918 between the British and the Americans, it was planned that the 'International' would be used by the French Army should the war have continued into 1919. The tank had new design features such as a separate engine compartment at the rear, and was built as one type only (as opposed to male or female versions). However, the end of the war meant only six entered British service, this example being the last remaining Mark VIII. The Americans had 100 such tanks completed, some of which stayed in service until the early 1930s for training purposes.

Mark IX

Another vehicle that did not see service before the war ended in November 1918, the Mark IX started life on the drawing board as a multi-purpose vehicle, but it was developed into an infantry carrier or supply vehicle. Nicknamed 'the Pig', it could take up to 30 soldiers into battle, or carry 10 tons of supplies and drag sledges behind carrying even more. The Mark IX was also used for flotation experiments in November 1918 at Hendon Reservoir.

Peerless Armoured Car

The need for armoured cars for internal security and 'policing' work around the world led the War Office to ask Austin to make armoured bodies of a design similar to what they had made for the Imperial Russian Government in the war. The British Army had a large number of American-made Peerless 2½-ton truck chassis in store, so 100 of these were supplied to Austin to have the armoured bodies fitted. The vehicle had duplicate steering controls at the rear to help it get out of 'tight spots'.

Rolls-Royce Armoured Car 1920 Pattern Mark I

The Royal Naval Air Service had first converted Rolls-Royce cars into armoured cars in late 1914 and the 'naval pattern' vehicle saw extensive use in the First World War. When the Army required a new armoured car the naval pattern was copied with few amendments. This vehicle saw service from 1920 to 1940 in locations as diverse as Ireland and Shanghai. As a testament to its build quality it still runs today at the museum's special events.

THE TANK MUSEUM

The Tank Museum at Bovington, Dorset, England, houses an international collection of over 300 vehicles, the best collection of armour anywhere in the world. Bovington was chosen as the location to train with the new tanks in 1916 and it has continued to be the home of British armoured vehicle training. The museum collection started as a teaching aid for soldiers and this role still remains, but the displays are now enjoyed by the general public, most of whom arrive with no prior knowledge of tanks. Regular live vehicle displays are held in the museum arena and talks, tours and demonstrations take place inside the museum daily. The museum also has a large Archive and Library – most of the images reproduced in this book have been sourced from the quarter of a million images held there.

Further details about the Tank Museum can be found at www.tankmuseum.org.

Appendix 2

Mark IV Tank Specifications

Crew	8
Weight	27.9 tons (28.4 tonnes)
Power-to-weight ratio	3.7bhp/ton (2.8kW/tonne)
Overall length	26ft 3in (8m)
Overall width (male)	13ft 6in (4.11m)
Overall height	7ft 11in (2.43m)
Engine	Daimler/Knight sleeve-valve, water-cooled straight-six, 105hp (78kW) @1000rpm
Transmission	Two-speed and reverse primary box with secondary two-speed selectors on output shafts
Fuel capacity	70gals (318 litres)
Max speed	3.69mph (5.95km/h)
Radius of action	35 miles (56km)

Fuel consumption	2.08gals/mile (5.9 litres/km)
Track pressure	27.8lb/sq in
Trench crossing	11ft 5in (3.5m)
Armour	1/2inch (14mm max)
Armament	2 x 6pdr 57mm 23-calibre quick-firing guns
	4 x .303 Lewis air-cooled machine guns
Max range (6pdr)	7,978yds (7,300m)
Muzzle velocity (6pdr)	1,348ft/sec (411mps)
Ammunition	Solid shot, high explosive, canister
Ammunition stowed (male)	332 x 6pdr, 6,272 x machine gun

Index

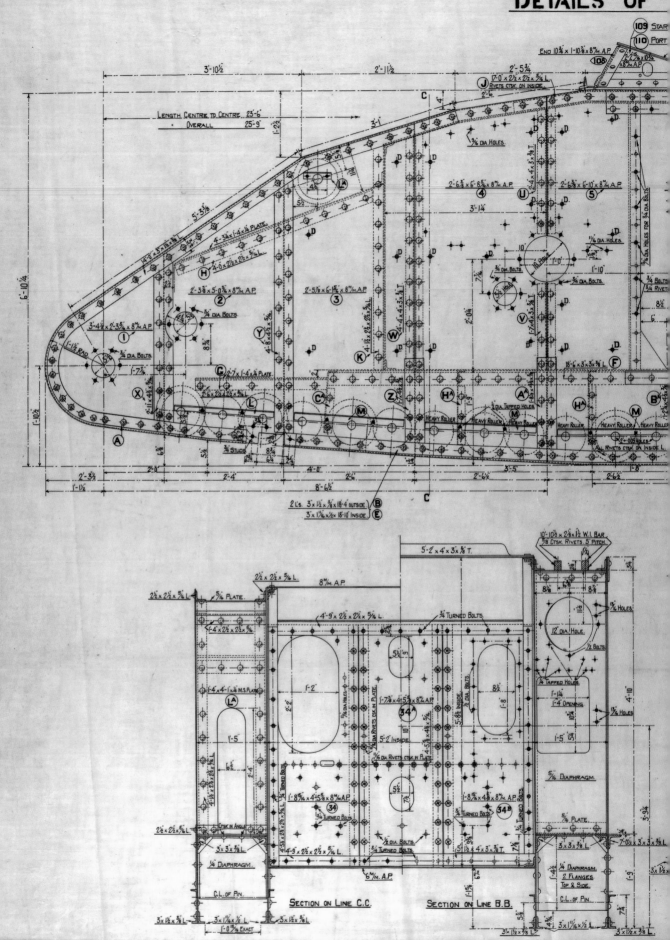